To

Thanks for all you have done + continue to do for our families!!

with love, Stacy

THE SOCIAL DIET

The 7 Essential Ingredients for Raising
Socially Connected, Well-Balanced and Caring Kids
(Especially Those with Social Learning Challenges)

Stacy Goresko Ph.D.

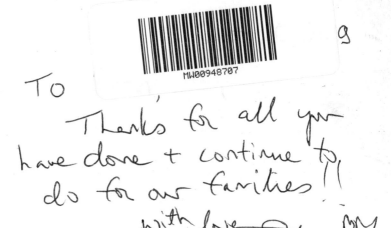

Author: Stacy Goresko, Ph.D.

Editors: Heather Harris-Bergevin, Amy Collette

Book Cover Design: Murrie Gayman, and Jenn Foster

Elite Online Publishing
63 E 11400 S #230
Sandy, UT 84070
www.EliteOnlinePublishing.com

Ordering information: Amazon.com *The Social Diet*

The Social Diet / Stacy Goresko, Ph.D. 1st ed.

ISBN: 978-1726799577

“Through the multiple lenses of parenting a child with autism, a Sociolinguist and other professional pursuits, Dr. Goresko has developed an understanding of the culture of autism, empowering her to support her son with a steady and enriching diet of skills and concepts to achieve success in the social world. Employing a developmental view of autism, this book is a must read for anyone seeking to better understand and educate people on the autism spectrum to engage in meaningful social interaction.”

-Stephen Mark Shore, Ed.D.

Internationally known Educator, Author, Consultant, and Presenter on issues related to the Autism Spectrum

Dedication

To Ylann and Yael,

Words cannot express the gratitude and deep love which I have for the two of you. Because of you, every day I choose to strive to be the best person I can be. You are my best teachers--you always have been, and you always will be! I know we have the signs up all over the house, but I will say it here for everyone to witness:

"Always Go After Your Dreams!

Life Is for The Taking…Go Grab It and It Will Be Yours!"

We will forever be one.

I love you,

Mom

Table of Contents

Prologue

A Note to the Reader:

My dream is that "The Social Diet" will become a household name, especially when it comes to raising our kids who struggle the most socially. In today's world of disconnection, I believe that every child needs a heavy Social Diet that brings families, societies, and nations together.

The intention of this book is to teach parents, caregivers, or anyone who loves a child how to connect with him or her on a deep level. My son was diagnosed with autism spectrum disorder (ASD) in 2003, at which point I directed all my focus to helping him and others. While I use examples from my work with this population, this book is also applicable to any child.

This book is not the typical book about autism, nor do I want it to be. My personal experience with parenting a child on the Autism Spectrum lead to my research, but this book is to assist people on all parts of the spectrum, and, I hope, any parent or caregiver of a non-neurotypical child can use the tools within these pages. There are so many books available about the Autism Spectrum and related disorders that I do not want to waste your time or repeat what you can easily find elsewhere, and that you're still searching for answers shows your dedication to your family. I want to give you the kind of information that *isn't* out there. I want to give you the information that people are *not* talking about but perhaps should.

The chapters which follow are a culmination of what I have learned over the past 15 years and want to share. I write to you as a mom of a child with autism, but also with the wisdom of a professional in the field. My job is to educate and empower you so you can make informed decisions and take thoughtful actions for your own child. A lot of what I have learned, both in my research and experience, is not in print elsewhere, as it comes from my own observations, perspectives, and personal trials and tribulations.

As a trained Sociolinguist, I look at the field of autism from a different perspective than many researchers. I see this as an asset. I hope that the information I've gathered for you helps you gain a new perspective, not just in interactions with non-neurotypical children, (whether your own or someone else's), but also with interpersonal communication for all individuals.

Introduction

The Social Diet® is for anyone who loves a child or adult with autism and related disorders. It is dedicated to the parents of these amazing children, and to all the compassionate and dedicated individuals who have chosen to work with and help them.

Chapter One, *A Letter from My Son,* exemplifies for me that even children with autism can be in touch with their feelings and speak from their hearts. It is also proof that The Social Diet® works. This is true not only with my own child, but with other families that I work with, and I hope for your family as well.

Chapter Two is my personal journey after my son's autism diagnosis. I focus on why my sociolinguistic brain honed-in upon what I call "the social piece." I explain why the social piece is the most important and neglected piece of the autism puzzle. This chapter reveals why we, as a culture, are not giving social learning the importance which it deserves. I point out how the current culture of autism gives way to certain cultural assumptions that, when examined closely, may be holding our children back from reaching their actual potential. I explain how sometimes our country's educational system has a myopic view towards special needs children, especially those who are twice exceptional. Here is my call for a reevaluation of our priorities and responsibilities to our children. I suggest the need to redefine what "success" looks like and call out for a (life) curriculum that supports this way of living and ultimately, point to the need for more relationship-based approaches. Here, I introduce The Social Diet®.

The Social Diet is made up of seven key ingredients. In the remaining chapters each ingredient is carefully explained so you can follow the "recipe" and put each of these into practice, immediately and easily to work for your family. At the end of each chapter I provide a section of reflection questions and practical exercises that you can try in your home in order to see the progression you desire.

I believe that The Social Diet will broaden your understanding of why we need to help our children become more social and the specific steps we can take to help them become more connected, more balanced and caring individuals. Social anxiety is very common amongst those with ASD, and the rules of cultural friendship practices which seem easily learned by some neurotypical individuals must be taught differently in homes where those cues are more difficult to learn. My vision is for every person to live a more social, meaningful, and connected life.

I cannot predict what anyone else's child will look like in the future. I can only give you the tools that have worked for me and for those families with whom I have consulted. I bring to you my passion and a fierce dedication to help you and your family in profound ways.

I know it may sound strange, but my son's autism diagnosis has been a gift. Despite the daily hardships, I am a better person and mother because of it. I no longer take the little things for granted. I cherish each baby step my son has taken. I have much more patience and empathy than I ever thought possible. Thanks to autism I was able to find the career of a lifetime. My family has also been affected in positive ways. Autism has brought a richness and appreciation of all people into my family's life and for that I am grateful. Together we touch and have been touched by the hearts of so many people. My life has been enriched, as I believe yours can be.

I hope that this book will touch the core of who you are as a parent. It is my intention to educate and empower families, as I do with private clients. As parents of special needs children, we need the courage to speak, get answers and have tools which make sense in our daily lives, in order to create solutions that work for your individual situation. It is an honor to bring The Social Diet to you, and I look forward to hearing from you.

Stacy Goresko

• CHAPTER 1 •

A Letter from My Son

I want to share with you a letter which I received from my son Ylann (pronounced Elon), who was diagnosed with autism at the age of 2. He wrote this Valentine's Day card to me when he was 12 years old, and is the reason I have chosen to write this book. The moment my son handed me this, it solidified the vision of what I had always known was possible in my child's social interactions. My son, and the work which I do daily, are testaments to every struggling parent, caregiver, and socially-challenged child that there is hope for a meaningful future of these children. The future is bright!

I invite all of us collectively, as a community in the broadest sense possible, to see that we are here not just to survive, but we are meant to *thrive*!

It is my heartfelt wish that all you moms and dads receive a letter like this from your child. It is pure, and from the heart and will forever touch me profoundly. As a parent, to receive a letter from my child, who was non-verbal until he was 4 old, and who has always had a great deal of struggle with interpersonal communication, meant that not only his mind and heart were thinking towards others in an empathetic way, but that his communication skills were improving. There were many struggles with handwriting and phrasing sentences, but he knew deep down that love and people are the most precious things we can give each other in life. Despite the many struggles he had (and there were many,) this letter was a pronouncement of the love he had for me and his family. For me it was (and still is) a forever gift. It was proof that all the efforts of living The Social Diet life were paying off and then some. When I read it, I feel that the world is good. I hope it can make your world better too.

Dear Mom,

In this world love is a fortune. As a nice, generous Mom you've been the best Mom in the world. For 12 long years you've taught me respect and discipline. For me being in the world, I was different. I had autism. You've been there for me and you've not sent me to that autism program that just would not help me. For 12 years you have the experience of being a great Mom. Mother, I credit you for these things: honesty, trustworthy, deployment as a parent, leadership, great parenting and a great soul. I love you so much that you have made love for me loving you. My love is always in your heart every day and you've been there for me. You have made me, Glen and Yael loving you. My tears are going to burst out for loving this card. I will always love you. Your love is a fortune!

Your son, Ylann Goresko

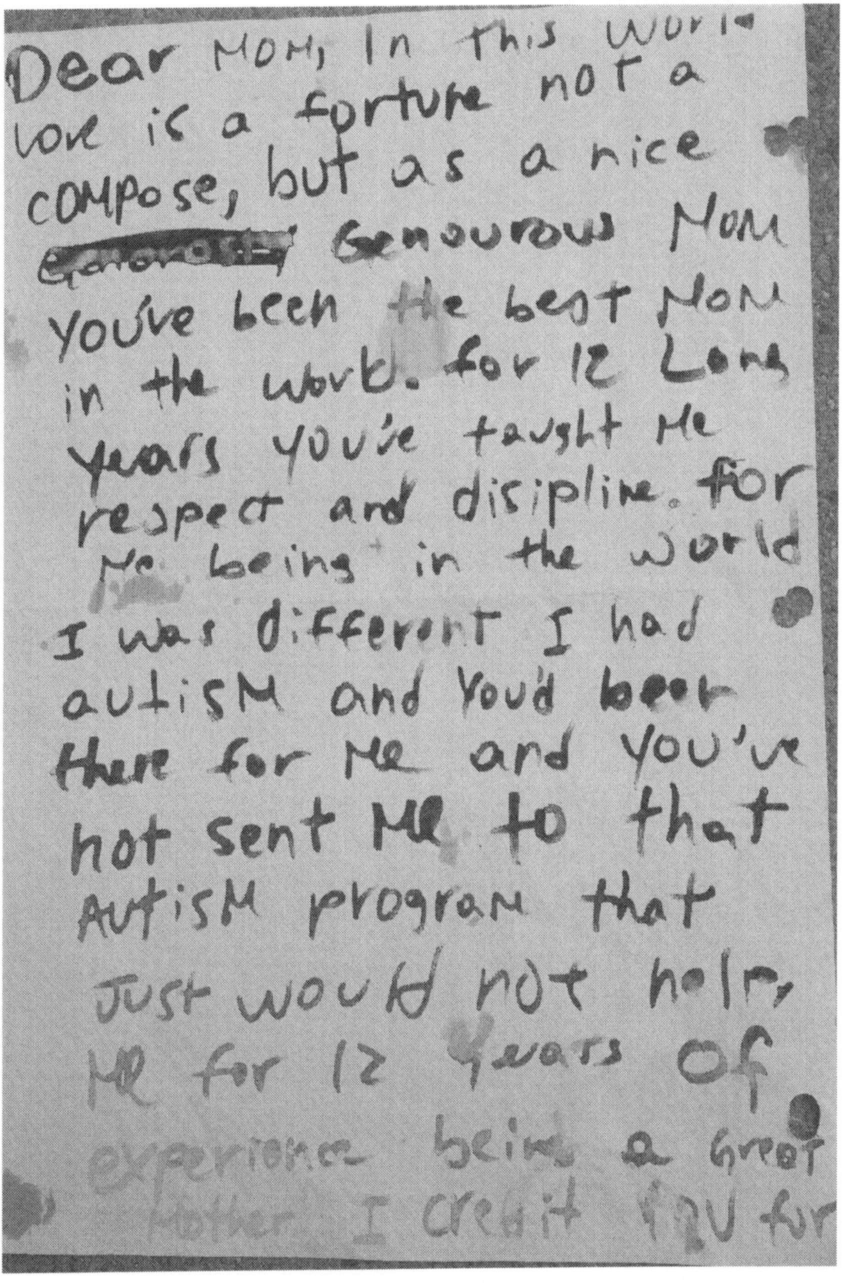

Dear MOM, In this world
love is a fortune not a
compose, but as a nice
Genourous Mom
you've been the best Mom
in the world. for 12 Long
years you've taught me
respect and disipline. for
me being in the world
I was different I had
autism and you'd been
there for me and you've
not sent me to that
Autism program that
just would not help
me for 12 years of
experience being a great
Mother. I credit you for

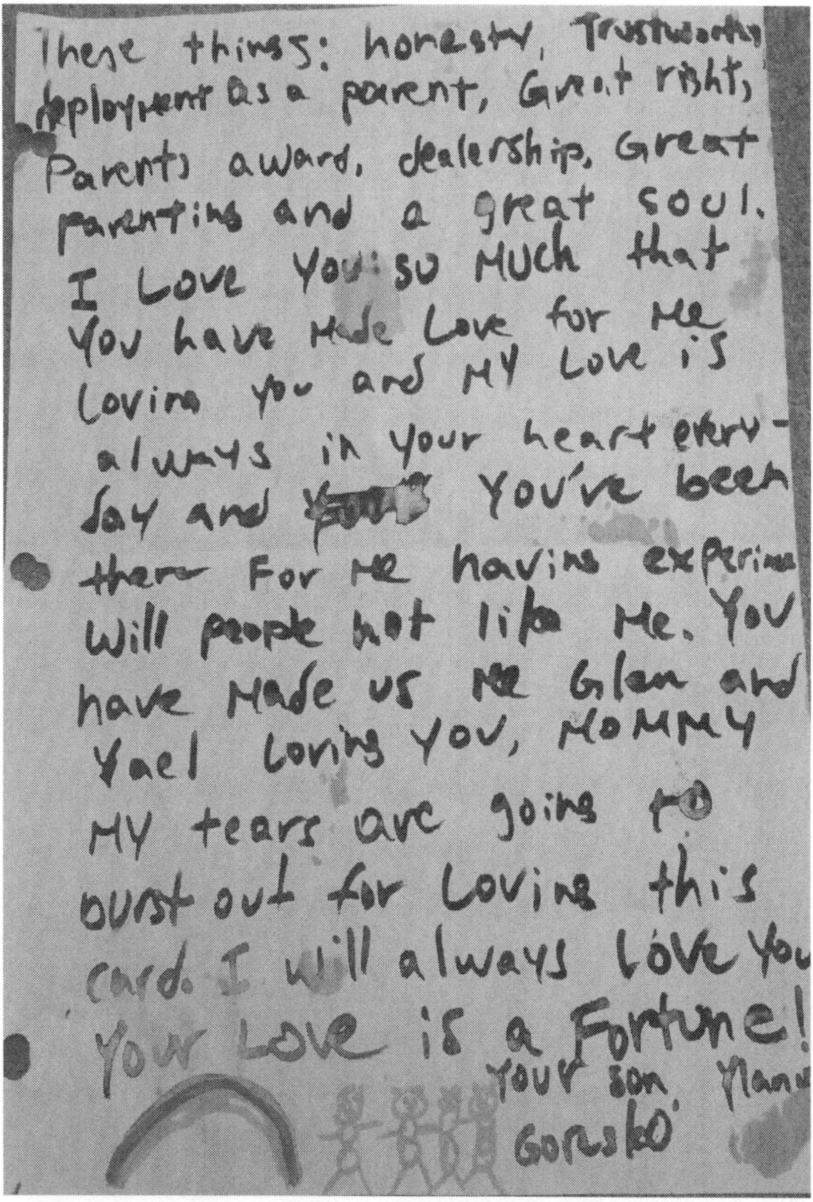

These things: honesty, Trustworthy
deployment as a parent, Great right,
Parents award, dealership, Great
parenting and a great soul.
I Love You so MUCH that
You have Made Love for me
Loving you and MY Love is
always in your heart everyday and You've been
there For me having experim
will people not like me. You
have Made us me Glen and
Yael Loving You, MOMMY
MY tears are going to
burst out for Loving this
card. I will always Love You
Your Love is a Fortune!
Your son Ylann
Gorsko

The Social Diet is what has allowed Ylann to write such a letter. As a family we have been practicing The Social Diet since Ylann was two-and-a-half years old. It grounded our family's way of thinking about autism and has become the foundation of our day-today life. It is the compass which guides me how to be the best parent for my child. It is the vehicle that has permitted my son Ylann to be able think for himself, problem-solve, connect to others, and learn to put others before himself. If you ask Ylann "What is the most important thing in life?" He will answer "To be a good person!" I did not know, when he was diagnosed, that my child could learn this, and I'm proud of him that he has-- not because he has memorized the phrase, but because together we strive to live this maxim, every day.

Like my son, I, too, speak from the heart. I always have, and always will. I know that there will be some naysayers out there, and I welcome that. My job is not to convince anyone. My job is to speak my truth—to speak about my path, what I have learned, and my desire to share it with you. I hope it touches, moves, and inspires you. If we, as families, can regain the portions of our children's potential, which we thought upon diagnosis had been lost forever—including a true connection with our children who struggle--it will have all been worth the fight.

• CHAPTER 2 •

The Story Begins...

I will never forget the feeling in my stomach, that first day. It felt as if someone had just kicked me in the belly and knocked the wind right out of me. I froze in place; I didn't know what to say, or what to think. All I can remember is thinking to myself, "This is bad. This is really bad." That was my only maternal gut instinct as I listened to the early childhood team who had just assessed my son and said, "*You might want to have Ylann evaluated to see if he has autism.*"

My 24-month-old, perfect boy... Autism? The evaluation team could see the look on my face as they tried to put into words a way to make me feel better. They said, "A lot of people with autism lead very productive lives, now. Many can learn how to drive a car, work, even get married!" I recall thinking at that moment, "Why are they telling me this?"

I was able to read between the lines. I understood that while some people on the spectrum might lead productive lives, others must not-otherwise why would they be saying this to my husband and me? Unable to help myself, I burst into tears. Now, all I could think about was the movie, "Rain Man." My son wasn't like Rain Man. He seemed so *normal*. To me, at least.

I could hardly muster up the words to respond. I just wanted to crawl into a hole and pretend this wasn't happening. An hour ago my son was, for all we knew, neurotypical. Now the professionals were suggesting that he has autism? The whole process was so surreal, with the benign medical professionals who did behavioral evaluations daily, parents grieving for a child who was sentenced to…what? As I sat there trying to wipe away the tears, I could hear myself mutter, "Pardon my ignorance, but what is autism?"

Here I was, a Ph.D. in Sociolinguistics, yet I didn't have a clue as to what autism was, outside of a few pop cultural references. Like many of us, I had vaguely heard of others with the diagnosis, and knew the numbers of diagnoses were increasing, but as it didn't apply to anyone in my family, I hadn't bothered to learn about it in detail. Quite frankly, I was scared of it, and felt confident that autism would be an area I would never have to ever think or worry about in my lifetime. I'm sure you understand.

My husband was supposed to drop me off at my office, but I knew I wasn't going to be able to do anything that day. I cried all the way home, in a daze, not knowing what to do or think. I do remember thinking, "How am I going to tell my family about this? *...By the way Mom, we found out today that Ylann probably has autism…*"

I spent the first couple of months after Ylann's diagnosis in mourning, disbelief, and was completely lost. I didn't want anyone to know that my beautiful baby had autism. I couldn't even say the word! It was a very dark period for me, those first six months or so. I look back now and am not sure how I got through that portion of the grief process, but I took it one day at a time and I learned to ask for help. I'm glad that I did, because without being willing to accept help, I might have gotten stuck in that grief process.

Now, close to 15 years later, I have a successful autism consulting practice. I travel all over the country giving workshops to parents and professionals, so that they can educate themselves, become empowered, and feel more in control of their lives, not despite their diagnosis, but being inspired by it. Autism will rob you of that illusion of control if you let it. The irony is, you have to be able to give up that illusion in order to make progress.

You must know, just as I did, right from the start, that autism is messy and complicated. It doesn't make sense. Every day is different. This is, I find, the beauty and nature of autism. We must learn to go with the flow, pick our battles and let other struggles go by the wayside.

I could not do that when I started on my journey. Now, I can look back at my own beginning mistakes, and offer you some hard-fought wisdom.

How The Social Diet® Began

I tell parents all the time, "There is good news, and there is not-so-good-news." The good news is that we know so much more about social and communication disorders (autism spectrum disorders, ADD/ADHD and dyslexia, to name a few) than we did 10 or 15 years ago. There are a plethora of options for treatment. The not-so-good-news is that these fields of study are relatively new, and the experts still do not have all the answers. On the contrary, professionals (myself included) are still far away from really understanding all the facets of social cognitive disorders and delays. So, where does this leave you? If the so-called "experts" don't have the answers, what do you do?

For myself, and in my work with parents with children on the spectrum, I found that we have to become our child's own experts. I found that if I wanted answers, and the professionals could not help me, I would have to educate myself, and become an informed consumer.

Even in those beginning months after diagnosis, one thing stood out for me, clear as day. Autism or no autism, my son *would* be social. My child would learn how to connect with others and have meaningful and long-lasting relationships. No one was going to tell me otherwise. This is something I felt very strongly about; I never wavered on it and I still don't. Being social was my North Star. Everything we did or didn't do in those early years was predicated on the following: *If it was going to make my child learn how to engage with others I gave it the green light. If there was a different agenda I politely said, "No thank you."*

I knew that general education skills could be learned at any age, but the social piece, that was another story. My Ph.D. in Education and Sociolinguistics (the study of face-to face verbal and non-verbal communication) had taught me that socialization in young children was critical to later mental development, and that should mean it was even more critical for non-neurotypical children. I knew that if Ylann was going to become socially integrated, then we were going to need professional support.

I found a speech therapist who understood that the foundation of any kind of life-learning needs to be embedded in social relationships. I found an occupational therapist who had the same philosophy. Then I stumbled upon Relationship Development Intervention→ (RDI→). RDI is a unique, relationship-based approach to treating autism spectrum disorders (ASD), and would change the course of my life, my son's life, and my career. I loved this model so much that I decided to get certified in RDI, and to become an RDI Program Certified Consultant.

Stephen Gutstein Ph.D., (founder and CEO of RDI), and I share common perspectives. His model trains consultants to be guides for the parents, so they can be guides for their children. In The Social Diet, I do the same thing. Dr. Gutstein's model focuses on processes, while I focus more on communication and family support, but our end goal is the same. My job, first and foremost, is to educate parents and other professionals about why the social piece is the most critical (after any medical concerns). I believe that every parent needs to understand how human interaction functions so that they can teach their children how to communicate and connect with others.

Second Language Learning and Autism

At that point in my career, I was not yet an autism professional. I was a French professor, and had spent many years studying foreign language classrooms and second language acquisition. Primarily, I studied which environmental factors enhanced or impeded second language learning. For example, I would go into classrooms and gather data on the percentage of the time spent on "teacher talk" vs. "student talk." I looked at the amount of time children were in whole group vs. small group activities. I studied who said what, to whom, how often, and what the outcomes were.

I set out to learn what made for optimal environments in second language learning, and, time and again, I found the same results created success. Classrooms where children were able to engage in genuine back-and-forth communication in the second language habitually made the most progress in learning that language. It wasn't the teacher; it wasn't the curriculum or skills taught which determined progress. It was, instead, the amount of time spent in real social engagement that made the difference. This makes sense, because if you want to learn a language, you must use it, and the more you are immersed in it, the better. Surprisingly, this bit of knowledge was overlooked in many classroom settings.

I think the most shocking statistic which I found was that on average, during a 45-60 minute class, each student had spoken in the second language for only *two* minutes. I found the same conclusions in the national literature which I was reading. In disbelief, I found myself saying, "No wonder we, as Americans, are so poor at learning languages, if we only get two minutes per day, 2-4 times per week, to actually practice and use the language." When I looked at it that way, I was amazed that anyone could learn a language in this environment, and in fact, most students do not. Research (and common sense) told me that in order to learn the language, you not only have to be *exposed* to it, but you need to be *engaged in* meaningful and authentic communication throughout the day, several times a week. The bottom line is that it's not enough to read it, write it, and hear it. You must also *experience* language and *use* it. There is no getting around this, if you want to be able to communicate in a real way.

What does learning a second language have to do with helping our children, especially those with autism? It turns out, a lot. I began to see important similarities among the two populations. In one, you have a population wanting to learn a second language. Students have to unlock the code (of language) and manipulate it in a real way, if they want to be a part of the foreign (to them) culture. It requires learning more than words, but requires the ability to adapt to a new way of thinking, and a new culture and, most difficultly, to integrate the two. Learning a second language takes the ability to absorb new material, but more importantly, it demands time and energy. The only way to learn a new language is to spend endless hours, weeks, months and even years to become an integrated, competent speaker. This can be physically and emotionally exhausting, and the first forays into the secondary culture, trying to figure out common practices, idioms, even the amount of body space necessary between speakers, can be a discomfiting experience.

Can't we say the same thing of a child who has autism? Don't they also need to break into a code and culture that is foreign to them? If this is the case, wouldn't studying this new and strange culture take a great deal of time and energy? Wouldn't it take years to become proficient in this foreign (to them) language and culture?

I found myself uttering, "Oh my God-- autistic kids have to do what we *all* have to do if we want to speak another language and become one with society." I thought to myself, "We have the research for success in first and second language acquisition—can't we just take that research and apply it to our autism population?" Of course, we can! A light bulb went on in my mind, and voilà: I had the answers I had been looking for. I knew exactly what my son and other autistic children needed to become proficient, participating members of our society and culture. Strangely, it was exactly the opposite of what happens with many non-neurotypical children, whose parents still bear the scars of the time prior to diagnosis, when going to church, to stores, and to school was fraught with judgmental glares from passersby and the general isolation which occurs when parenting a "different" child.

The answer, of course, was total immersion. Ylann needed to be totally immersed in our culture, our community, our family, our life. The Total Immersion method is also known as the Sink or Swim method for learning languages, which comes from the language acquisition research. Very broadly speaking, my research shows that the fastest way to learn a second language is to immerse yourself within it. Immersion is also the preferred methodology to retain the new language being taught. The premise is simple and logical: if you want to learn a new language or culture, spend time *participating* or engaging with native speakers. The more time spent in active, real-time communication and authentic situations, the faster, better, and more permanent that learning will become.

Immersion Approach

When we see the connection between language acquisition and autism, we can understand the monumental task which lies in front of parents and their children. Neurotypical children learn how to communicate and participate almost instinctually. Even though it takes years for them as well, they don't have to work as diligently at this social learning, because it often comes naturally. But, for our kids with developmental delays, this is not always the case. Providing this population with immersion settings is not easy, but if you are ready to do the hard work and have a fierce determination to make this a top priority for you and your child, The Social Diet will provide you with the seven essential ingredients to do so. It will require you to have an open mind. Initially it might require you to go beyond your comfort zone, especially if you, too, are non-neurotypical, and this technique was not used in your childhood home. It will require you to speak up and advocate for your child. It will require you to look at your own life, beliefs and values, in order to make the necessary changes which make it possible to live by those value and beliefs. It might even require you to redefine your definition of success for yourself and your child, and learn new paths to how your family can live a more connected and meaningful life. If you are wanting your child to be immersed in real life and take it on, The Social Diet will give you the recipe to do this and more.

Reflection and Questions:

- Think back to your years in school. How were you taught a second language?
- Was it meaningful? How far were you able to go using the language?
- Did you reach proficiency or fluency? Why or why not? If you are one of the lucky few who did reach fluency, what were the factors that made the difference for you? If you never became proficient, why do you think that is?
- Speak to a person who is fluent in another language. Ask them how they became fluent. Ask them how much time it required to feel a part of the new language's community and culture? Did it happen overnight? Or did it take years?
- Now imagine that you want your child to become fluent in your language and culture so they can become as integrated as you are. How many years did it take you? How long can you expect it will take your child? What would be your guess as to how many hours per day and per week would you need to spend on this for it to happen?

• CHAPTER 3 •

The Autism Culture

If you are reading this book, you or someone you care about is most likely a member of what I call "The Culture of Autism." I use the term "culture" in an anthropological sense. From this perspective a *culture* is "a way of life of a group of people—the behaviors, beliefs, values and symbols that they accept, generally without thinking about them, and are passed along by communication and imitation from one generation to the next."[1]

We are all members of various cultures, whether we realize it or not. Most of us belong to a family culture. Throughout our education, we probably have been part of a school culture. Those of us who subscribe to a certain religious orientation belong to that culture. Wherever there are groups of people, we find culture. So, even though most of us never stop to think about it, there is a definite and distinct autism culture in this county.

As parents, we need to recognize that there is indeed a strong *culture of autism* which exists in this country, and which is historically based. This culture has a strong bias which dictates how we think, practice and treat Autism Spectrum and related disorders.

---

[1] Choudhury, Ifte. http://people.tamu.edu/~i-choudhury/culture.html

In this chapter, I will take an in-depth look to see how the autism culture makes certain assumptions which may be false, and which can lead to cultural blind spots that affect our children's social outcomes. I also want to discuss potential obstacles which our children face at school, and what you as the parent can do about those pitfalls. My goal is to educate and empower you, so that you can make more empowered decisions about the kinds of services you want for your children. That begins with the historical perspective.

How my Role as a Sociolinguistic Helps Inform Me About The Autism Culture

My role as a behaviorist is very different from others who call themselves behaviorists. While it is true that we share the same job title *what* we actually do, specifically what we study and *how* we study it, differs. In Psychology, all behaviorists study behavior, and what influences behavior, but our approaches are different and our methods of intervention are different. While each of us falls under the same category of "Behavioral Services," what I do as a Sociolinguistic Behaviorist differs greatly from those who are trained as traditional Behaviorists, aka Applied Behavior Analysts.

Traditional Behaviorist Approach

The treatment of autism spectrum disorders (ASD) was developed from a perspective known as *behaviorism*. The roots of behavior therapy extend back to the late 1800s / early 1900s with the work of Russian physiologist **Ivan Pavlov** (1849 – 1936). Behavior therapy didn't become an established form of psychological treatment until the 1950s.

Traditional behavioral therapy sought to find out what people do (their actions) and why they do it. Behaviorists believe that actions are determined, either reinforced or extinguished, by consequences, either positive or negative. The general idea is that if we study what people *do* and *why* they do it, we can then change their behaviors by changing the environmental factors causing those behaviors.

In 1938, B.F. Skinner, one of the most famous social scientists, formulated the "*law of reinforcement*." This law stipulated that "A behavior followed by a reinforcer will increase (that behavior) in probability." Skinner believed that all behavior is "operant," or conditioned, since it "operates" on the environment involved, or is controllable by the individual.[2] In other words, people learn to behave a certain way, either positively or negatively, based on extrinsic motivators, motivators outside of themselves.

The field of behavior analysis has developed many techniques for increasing useful behaviors and reducing those that may cause harm or interfere with learning. Applied behavior analysis (ABA) is the use of these techniques and principles to bring about meaningful and positive change in behavior. The principles and methods of ABA

---

[2] Skinner, B.F. *The behavior of organisms: an experimental analysis,* New York: Appleton-Century, 1938

have helped and still help many different kinds of learners acquire many different skills—from leading healthier lifestyles to the mastery of new languages.

Since the 1960's, professionals have been applying behavior analysis in order to help individuals with autism and related developmental disorders. To a large degree, this application has been successful. Without a doubt, ABA has been instrumental in getting people with autism to learn to act in certain ways, and/or to learn certain skills or desirable behaviors. Today, ABA is still recognized as the most popular method for autism treatment.

My job as a Sociolinguistic

My job as a Sociolinguist is not grounded in applied behavioral theory, however. The principles and methods of my approach are derived from anthropology, and the field of verbal and nonverbal communication. My work in sociolinguistics is very similar to what an anthropologist does. Take, for example, the anthropologist Jane Goodall, who researched and studied chimpanzees. Unlike many other researchers in her time, Goodall did not study her subjects from afar, and she did not only rely on book knowledge to educate herself about them. Instead, she lived with her subjects, in the midst of the forest, integrating herself within the chimpanzee troupe. She immersed herself with the population of great apes, and by doing so she got an up close and personal understanding of their culture and communication. In the field of anthropology, there is a term for someone whose job it is to observe and participate in a culture other than one's own: they are known as Ethnographers.

Sociolinguists are like anthropologists because we, too, are ethnographers who immerse ourselves into a culture to get an insider's perspective of how the group lives. Our role is the same as an anthropologist, but our focus is specifically upon communication. We study the culture of human behavior in terms how communication (the verbal and non-verbal behavior of a group of people) informs us about how a culture thinks and acts. Sociolinguists study how people's thinking and behavior is embedded into specific cultural beliefs and values. This means that we study how particular cultures use verbal and non-verbal communication at the macro (big picture) level and how the macro culture informs and reflects people's communication at the micro (individual) level.

Both anthropologists and sociolinguists understand that behavior is patterned. Our job is to get the broad brushstrokes of a culture's behavioral patterns while, at the same time, to see how these patterns may enhance or impede members' quality of life in the culture being studied.

As a Sociologist, my job over the past several years has been to study the autism culture. During this time, I was able to uncover certain patterns of behavior in how we, as a culture, talk about and treat autism, in a global sense. I was able to figure out the communication patterns of what people were saying and how their behaviors matched their thinking. Once I had an accurate insider's perspective on this, I then studied how these patterns of behavior filtered down into the many standard general practices found in schools and in-home programs.

By studying the macro/micro relationships and the micro/macro relationships, I was able to study the cultural underpinnings—the values and beliefs that were found in treatment models.

Autism Culture in Schools

As I visited more schools, it became obvious to me quickly that ABA was the treatment model of choice in almost every instance. It was everywhere. I did not have to do much digging to find out that ABA enjoys a privileged status in the field of treating non-neurotypical children in general, and in autism treatment in specific. ABA recommendations are all I heard about, then, and still. As soon as I got my son's diagnosis, doctors and other parents sounded the alarm: "Ylann needs between 20-40 hours of ABA per week!" That was all they had to offer. I didn't hear about anything else. Everyone I talked to was saying the same thing, over and over: ABA therapy is the only route we know of to help your child. I remember thinking, "What is this ABA I keep hearing about? Why is everyone telling me we need to do this?" I was no different than any other new caregiver to a non-neurotypical child: if the professionals told me Ylann needed it, I was compelled to look it up.

I didn't blindly follow the crowd. I wanted to do my homework and understand why ABA therapy was so popular. I became very curious about why ABA was so pervasive. Surely there would have to be other approaches for the treatment of ASD. Common sense told me that there cannot be a "one size fits all" solution —not for something as complex and with such varied symptomology as autism. But, no matter where I went, no matter what I studied, the discourse was unbelievably the same throughout the country. Apparently, there is a strong bias and buy-in for using an ABA to teach and train those with autism.

The Difference Between Applied Behavior Analysis and Behavior Modification.

After doing some investigation, I began to realize that Applied Behavior Analysis did make a lot of sense to me and is certainly a sound scientific methodology to the treatment of Autism Spectrum Disorders. I also learned of an approach called Behavior Modification, which is not the same thing as ABA, yet a lot of people think they are. I learned that before the 1980's, Behavior Modification was synonymous to ABA, which was confusing at first. There are still many people who believe that they are the same. Parents and professionals, though, need to know about their differences. If you look up various definitions of Behavior Modification online and in dictionaries, you will see that most of them reference reward, punishment, and decreasing desired behaviors. They often discuss this as synonymous with "behavior therapy" and mention that behavior modification techniques were common in the 1970's and 1980's. This is all true.

The difference between behavior modification and "applied behavior analysis" however, is that anyone with minimal training can use behavior modification techniques, and there is no legal repercussion. There is no certification board governing who can say they practice behavior modification. There is high variability in people who may have gotten a few courses, or watched a workshop and read books, and now call themselves a "behaviorist" or behavior therapist. This comes with a lot of risks, obviously, so you will want to investigate how qualified your potential provider really is.

Behavioral Modification is still practiced, by some people who call themselves "Behaviorists", but NOT practiced by people who are actually "applied behavior analysts," as behavior modification techniques are antiquated. Applied behavior analysts analyze all behavior *before* intervening. In fact, applied behavior analysts use many different types of interventions to change subtle behaviors identified by the client themselves that they want to change or learn or to impact outcomes decades down the road. Behavior Modification uses *artificial* positive and negative reinforcement to increase desired behaviors and/or to extinguish or reduce undesirable behaviors. Behavior Modification uses reward and punishment, whereas ABA does not.

It is important to note that *rewards* are not the same things as *reinforcers*. If a parent learns her child is being exposed to a program espousing "rewards and punishment", this is not ABA. By definition, in behavior analysis, a reward is not something that actually increases behavior (more about this later in the chapter.) Science shows that a reward is just something arbitrary given to try to get someone to do something, or given after someone does something a caregiver wants to see increase. This is something behavior modification uses a lot, but a true behavior analyst would not. A reinforcement is a *natural* phenomenon. It happens in the natural environment. For example, if a baby smiles a social smile for the first time, and nobody responds (such as in my clients from abusive and neglectful situations), he quickly loses that instinct to continue smiling socially. But, if a baby smiles and mom is delighted, and coos and aahs and smiles back, it continues. They use this amazing dance of smiling at each other that has now begun and is strengthened, as the reinforcement. The baby experienced something that is "reinforcing."

I think it's fair to say that ABA is scientifically sound, whereas Behavior Modification may not be. It would be important when you are choosing a methodology that you recognize the difference. Behavior analysis, by definition, must have social validity. If you see a program calling itself ABA but there is no social validity, it's not actually ABA. Also, true applied behavior analysts do no need to use punishments as reinforcers. The problem is that there are many professionals who claim to be using ABA in their practice but are not. I have seen this more times than I care to mention. Often, ABA gets a bad reputation because it is misrepresented as Behavior Modification.

Parents, use caution when it comes to choosing providers for your family. I tell potential clients to steer clear of anyone who thinks that their method is the best and will solve all of their child's challenges.

This would be wonderful to find, but it simply does not exist. None of us (myself included) could ever possibly have all the answers for something as complex as autism spectrum disorder or anything close to this. If an outfit sounds too good to be true, it probably is. We, as consumers, need to be vigilant and educate ourselves, so that we are clear and armed with the variety of diverse tools we will need along the journey.

That being said, ABA is the only model that is talked about and practiced in our public schools, in specialized schools/organizations, and in-home programs, with very few exceptions. It is also the only method which is funded by our government. Yet, I have witnessed poor practices in schools that claim to be using ABA but are not.

When I was first doing my research, I couldn't help wondering why ABA was so overtly accepted as the first and last stop for the treatment of ASD. Yes, like I noted above, ABA is based on scientific proven research and for that it should be revered. I am not disputing this. What I do dispute is the lack of discourse about *other* methodologies besides applied behavior analysis, which are worth studying and knowing. I worry about a culture which has chosen "The" most popular approach at the expense of entertaining other sound models, to the point where we close doors on each other without a rigorous understanding of what others might bring to the table. I can't tell you how many doors have closed on me before they even met me. The brief and concise comment goes something like this. "Are you a BCBA (Board Certified Behavior Analyst), because that is all we do, and that is the only way we can pay you. So even though it what you do sounds great, we just can't use you." I walk away not knowing more about them, they walk away not knowing what gifts I bring. Again, when it comes to something as significant as ASD, where it really does take a village, closing doors on one another, without being able to think outside the box together, is more than worrisome. As a community, we have got to fight back against this kind of mentality. Separatism is bad, yet more and more this is where I see the field going. For the sake of our children, I ask that we put away our myopic lenses, long enough to have a dialogue with one another as human beings. We have come to a point that we are so quick to point fingers, so quick to judge, so quick to make decisions without taking the time to even be curious about what or how different perspectives and different approaches might add more richness and bring about stronger outcomes. We are all better off together than separate. We have to fight back.

Parents, you need to start this movement. As much as ABA works, and does change people's lives, no one approach should dictate over the other. Nor should those of us who, like myself, are very gifted in other ways, not be considered legitimate. We are all losing out here. I fear that young people entering the field only think about working as an applied behavior analyst, because that is all that is talked about and, therefore, that is all they know about. If we just took the time to be open-minded and inquisitive, we could change our children's world. It's as simple as picking up Dr. Stephen

Shore's and Linda G. Rastelli's book *Autism for Dummies*[3] to realize the plethora of other sound methodological choices. I worry when a government decides for us what we should be doing for *our* children guising itself as the all-knowing chosen one, as each of our neurologically different children has varied needs. As well intentioned as this single methodology approach might be, this is more than alarming to me, and it should be for you.

Please don't misunderstand me. It is not a question of proving which or why one treatment model is any better or worse than another. I do *not* espouse an either/or approach to the treatment of ASD. In fact, I believe quite the opposite. My point is that, as a field, we should welcome different models and work together, not against each other. A collaborative approach brings richness and more rigor to our children. Again it is very worrisome that we live in a culture of "my way is better than your way," and in fact, "I don't want to even talk to you because we practice....(fill in the blank), and you practice something else." I fear the autism professionals are becoming clone-like, with Applied Behavior Analysis at the top looking down at anything or anyone else. No matter where I go in the country, when I walk into any public school, the discourse and behavior of those in charge and those teaching is exactly the same. Uniformity, of course, does serve a purpose (to an extent), but this "one size fits all" should not prevail across our nation. Where is the

---

[3] Autism for Dummies, Dr. Stephen Shore and Linda G. Rastelli, Wiley Publishing Inc., Hoboken, N.J. 2006.

diversity of thought? Where is the healthy bantering that we all should a part of? Where is the tolerance, the freedom for families not to be swayed one way or another? To me as a Sociolinguist, we are treading in dangerous waters.

Why is ABA so popular?

Besides the reasons I have stated above, one day, after several years of searching for answers, I figured out why ABA therapy protocols are so popular. The answer is so obvious, yet it took a long time before I figured it out: ABA is so pervasive because it mirrors our own standard, neurotypical American culture. ABA mimics the values and the belief systems that we already have in place. It is familiar, and we've already seen it work in child development situations. The similarities are unquestionable. ABA is so popular because it makes sense *to us.* The underlying principles of what makes Americans successful are the same principles that are taught to our autism population.

Every culture has its shared values and beliefs. When I realized that ABA borrows directly from the shared American culture I began to unravel the reasons ABA enjoys its gold-standard status.

Cultural Assumptions

When I look at autism from a cultural standpoint, it appears to me that our community is entrenched in a certain kind of thinking and behaving. We are so accustomed to and acculturated to think and act a certain way, that we may not even think to question it. This is especially true when we have been raised within an culture that reinforces certain beliefs and values systems that we mistakenly hold as "truths," not recognizing that there are other cultural norms in other societies, some of which seem very strange to our culture.

The best example that illustrates this point is a true story. I was working for a client in a big metropolitan state. The parents had a daughter with significant autism, and had flown me in to evaluate her school and classroom situation, in order to see if it was well suited for her needs at the time. After I entered her classroom, it didn't take me long to assess the class climate. They used a very traditional outdated model, where emphasis is placed on learning *skills* rather than learning how to *relate and connect* with others. It was immediately clear to me that this child spent all of her time at school trying to memorize the information which she thought the adults were asking her to learn, and she had no sense of what she was learning or why she was learning it. Her school life revolved upon rote memorization. Even with a significant cognitive delay, she was able to understand that as long as she got the "right" answer that the adults were looking for, and was able to repeat that same answer several times (enough for it to be data worthy), she could go on and do something which she wanted. In other words, she got rewarded for her behavior—what she did or did not do, what she said or did not say.

Three things were obvious to me. First, the professionals called this "learning," and were pleased with her "progress." Second, they had "proof" that this was learning because they had the "data" to prove it. As long as she came up with the requested answer, she was "learning" and they were doing their jobs. Third, she could have no idea what she was saying or why she was learning, but that was okay under this system, because she gave them the "right" answer. Clearly, changes needed to be made.

My recommendation was to pull her out of this school and put her into one that was more relationship-based. The school disagreed with my decision, for various budgetary reasons. You see, she was in a public school, which didn't require the district to pay more than they would have to for any student. If they agreed that the more social setting was more appropriate, the district would have to pay more money for this child, since the new school was not public.

Cultural Assumption Number 1:

"Evidence-Based" Treatments are the only treatment that should be used to treat ASD"

The first assumption in the autism culture is that only evidence-based models should be used to treat Autism Spectrum Disorders. Evidence-Based Practice (EBP) is a catchy term that we see everywhere in the research and in practice. "Evidence-based practice is a process that brings together the best available research, professional expertise, and input from youth and families to identify and deliver services that have been demonstrated to achieve positive outcomes for youth, families, and communities." [4]

It is logical that our autism culture would want to offer methodologies that are "evidence-based." Evidence-based approaches are now mandated, even by governmental and school agencies. In fact, it seems that any approach or methodology that is to be used in public school or in the private sector must be evidence-based. What parent wouldn't want their child's treatment to be evidence-based? But wait, maybe there is more to it than meets the eye. Allowing only EBP methodologies may be short-sighted.

I ask all parents to be discriminating consumers. I am not disputing that evidence-based models are proven to be effective. *Of course,* they are, or they wouldn't be the labeled as such. However, I do think we are overlooking something important.

Allow me to explain.

No treatment is deemed "evidence-based" until someone uses it, documents it works, and publishes a peer reviewed paper in an accepted medical journal saying that it has been used, and does work in the intended population. One prime example is the PEERS [5] curriculum. Initially they didn't yet have the studies behind them to warrant the EB title. But then, they were used by hundreds, and they

---

[4] www.acf.hhs.gov/sites/default/files/fysb/evidencebasedpractice20120829.pdf

[5] Leaf, Justin; Leaf, Jeremy A.; Milne, Christine; Taubman, Mitchell; Oppenheim-Leaf, Misty; Torres, Norma; Townley-Cochran, Donna; Leaf, Ronald; McEachin, John; Yoder, Paul (2017). An evaluation of a behaviorally based social skills group for individuals diagnosed with autism spectrum disorder. *Journal of Autism and Developmental Disorders, 47 (2),* 243-259.

DID work and now they ARE evidence based. The same can be said for The Social Diet. While I respected a lot of what I saw, I choose RDI for my family, and I think it is wonderful, as do most who used this approach. Yet, those of us who espouse RDI are used to the backlash of others insisting that the research is not there. At the time, for my family, it made the most sense. I was confident enough to know that in the end, it has to make sense to *me*, the parent because it is my child.

I ask you to use your common sense. Sometimes by the time something warrants the BP seal of approval, your child, who was once four years old, now is eight and you may have lost four precious years because you wanted to wait for the school system or physicians to stand behind a particular methodology they have established as the only way. This is foolish and unnecessary. Educate yourself and you decide what balance of therapies is best for your child. Make your own sound decisions after a lot of thoughtful reading, digging, searching, watching.

Be weary of treatments that are not designed to address the "Big Questions"

It is important to choose treatment models that are designed to address life's long-term goals, such as having a loving, fulfilling and meaningful life. The "*big* questions," are the ones which keep parents awake at night. In the long run parents are not so worried that their child receives an "A" on a math test or that their child isn't toilet trained. I don't mean to imply these are not issues, but they don't warrant the same amount of concern as the overall "*big questions*" do concerning our children's quality of life when they are older. We know that some therapies can cause a child to seem acceptable to a certain extent in our culture and society. We, however, are barely gathering the information needed for long term studies reaching into decades of information, how autism progresses and can intensify in adulthood, and whether the management techniques that were acquired in childhood comes at the cost of long term happiness.

All parents (especially parents with children who are on the Autism Spectrum, or who are non-neurotypical in some way) cannot help but worry about what their child's future will look like. The "BIG Questions" that keep us up at night are as follows:

- What kind of life will my child have?
- Will my child ever be able to be in committed relationships?
- Will my child be able to think independently and have the mental maturity for real life?
- Will my child be able to successfully hold down a job and be self-supporting?
- Will my child be able to have a fulfilling life and be happy?
- Will my child be able to become an integral part of the community?

- Will my child ever be able to get married, *stay* married, and have children?

In my opinion, it is these kinds of *big* overarching questions which need to drive the conversation and be included in our autism interventions. How do we come up with EBP for this line of forward thinking? This is no easy task, but does that mean we shouldn't be working on it or choose approaches like The Social Diet which are grounded within the long-term quality of life issues? I hope not, for the sake of our children.

Some constructs are not and never were designed to address these bigger, long-term life questions. Some are not interested in designing methods that *can*not be "quantitatively measured." The Social Diet, in contrast, is designed as a qualitative application, because that is the way life is. I question our culture's need to perpetuate scientifically qualitative data over quantitative interventions because it makes little sense to rely solely on skills-based models for the treatment of primarily socially-based disorders.

The following questions make up the underlying framework principles of The Social Diet's goals for learning. It would not be in our children's best interests to have their treatment methodologies exclude the following, yet many do- even those deemed evidence-based. You want to choose an approach that can answer a resounding "Yes" to the following questions regarding any given methodology.

- Does it make our children feel significant?
- Does what we do make them feel important and special?
- Does it support them in a loving environment, where they feel safe, respected, accepted and honored?
- Does it challenge them in a way that is motivating and developmentally appropriate?
- Are the people who support them authentic, and is the approach or content they are teaching authentic and applicable to the here and now (as opposed to a staged or contrived environment)?
- Does the methodology emphasize and require interacting with others while, at the same time, promote their higher level cognitive problem-solving and flexible thinking processes?
- Do children spend at least 20 (and preferably 40) hours per week in real time face-to-face engagements where they are required to collaborate with others, which uses their cognitive processing, flexible thinking, and problem-solving part of their brain?
- Do they have ample opportunities to engage in new experiences (that are purposely not routine) and new people throughout their day, several times a week? (While a certain amount of routine is needed, a good portion of their day should be spent learning new ways to adapt to new

experiences and new people just like they will need to do in real life. We are not doing them any favors by allowing them to stick to rigid schedules or activities they may like, but which may be counter-productive in the long run.)

- Are they being continuously challenged in a way that is *just beyond* their current level of learning?
- Are they exhibiting and incorporating spontaneous, appropriate emotions, in real time?
- Are they making genuine connections with real people in their lives, in a way that can only be intrinsically learned and felt?
- Does the therapy use an intrinsic model for discovering childrens' own motivation for learning? Be sure to ask potential providers lots of questions, making sure they do in fact include all the points mentioned above. If they answer "Yes," probe even further and ask them how they do this and can they give you some examples. Then ask if you can sit in one of their sessions to observe them in action. (You will have to get together the proper consent forms, first.)

Cultural Assumption Number 2:

Skill-Based Learning is Enough, and is All That is Needed:

The Problem with Skill-Based Models of Learning

Skill-based learning will never teach you how to thrive as a human being. It is expedient, I agree. We all are byproducts of its benefits. I know that I learned my math basics (addition, subtraction, multiplication and division) via the card drills that I had in elementary school, as did we all. I memorized those suckers, and they are hard wired in my brain now for all time! Rote skills certainly have their place in the education system, especially when it comes to memorizing needed repetitive information which has a specific function. I totally agree with this, and do not want you to think that I am saying there is no place for these important learning tools or memorization. Think about how you learned how to type, play a musical instrument, how to work your iphone-- if you need to ingest material for something or someone that is needed quickly and without much reflection once it is memorized, a skill-based, repetitive method works best.

There is one big problem with this, however. Learning what it is to be human, the wonderfully complex intricacies of our social emotional world, can never be learned, or understood only by memorization of information which one is given. As humans, we have to *participate* and *experience* the interactive dance that only human beings are privileged to delight in. There is no textbook, no memorized material that can come close to the emotions that we humans feel at any given time.

Our modern-day autism culture would have us believe that academic and skill-based learning is all that we need to succeed in life, but we, as adults, know that this cannot be true. If that were true our kids could simply learn skills, and get good grades, which would then afford them a life filled with purpose and connectedness. Wouldn't that be magnificent? Once again, however, this is not how real life works. This assumption mirrors our America's "buy in" culture of *product* oriented thinking, rather than *process* oriented conclusions.

Skill-based learning does give our kids *skills*, and this is not a bad thing. Goodness knows, they need these skills to function in society in adulthood, and to hold jobs. However, these skills do not teach them how to relate to other people, and how to implement these skills in the ever-changing, complex environment we live in. The founding fathers of behavioral analysis were the first to have broken down human behavior into discrete skills which can be taught, learned, and measured and therefore putting it on the map of scientific practices. …but something was, and still is, missing. The sum of the parts (skills) acquired does not, in adulthood, give us a complete human being. I believe, in contrast, that skills training gives us only skills. Who is teaching our children about life beyond the skills which they need in order to function appropriately within an active, changing culture? I don't see much of a skill-based curriculum which addresses this.

Yes, your child might be able to get dressed on his own but what about when it's winter and he puts on shorts and a tee shirt and wants to go outside without boots, coat or a hat, you still have a problem. The task of "dressing himself" can be checked off on the data sheet to show "evidence" that he has mastered this task, but to what effect?

The skill in and of itself isn't helpful, if it isn't accompanied by the child's understanding of *why* we do certain things. Many parents face these behaviors in their toddlers and preschoolers, but their neurotypical (NT) children learn quickly from social cues and observation of others in their surroundings. This is not always the case in our non-neurotypical (non-NT) children.

The same can be said for speech acquisition. Ylann's speech therapist once told me this, and it makes complete sense. I can get a child to say words, but words in and of themselves don't mean anything, if there is no connection to what the words mean and how to use them in real life. A lot of you know what I am saying, especially if you deal with instances of echolalia with your child. Your child might be verbal, but speech is not an accumulation of memorizing a list of words or phrases. Speech was always meant as a means of communication as a process, in order to connect with people.

A good example of this came from a mother of a former client. One day she turned to me and said, "I believe you now. You were right. We spent so much time worrying about Speech, whether it will come, or not come. But the truth of the matter is, it will come if it's going to come. But being social-- being able to make a friendship and being able to play-- is so much more important. Now that he's bigger, it's really hard to roll back the time and find the friendships we could have found more easily when he was younger." She continued with "I couldn't see it, I didn't want to see it. Now, I think he would have talked, even if we didn't spend so much time on Speech therapy trying diligently to get him to talk."

Why do we see so many skill building techniques, rather than more socially based learning? One reason I believe this to be true is that it is hard to measure a non-skills based curriculum, which, perhaps, is why traditional constructs do not address these more complex concerns. It is much easier to look at the kinds of behavior and discrete skills that are clearly measurable. We call it "successful" because the skills are mastered and there is evidence that this has occurred, in nice neat charts and behavior forms. The success that skill-based data measures is a child's success at completing a task.

Let me say, I know how difficult it is for our children to complete and master tasks, whether from executive function difficulties, or other communications concerns, or merely from the comorbidity of attention and communication processing disorders with Autism. I am not in any way trying to downplay the importance of our children learning to toilet train, pick up messes, make beds, or drive cars. Obviously, these things are critical steps towards the goals we, as adults, have in mind for them to be as independent as possible in adulthood. However, completing a task is relatively easy in comparison to having to learn how to become a responsible and connected human being, something many neurotypical adults struggle with as well. What, then, about those aspects of human *beings* that defy discrete measurement? Do we simply ignore them because they are too messy to deal with? Do we simply not put them into our equation, because we can't a find clear-cut, evidence-based methodology to back it up?

Granted, this is a tricky business, and I realize this is not as straightforward as a skill-based model. But we can't ignore that humans are complex, complicated creatures that need to be nurtured. We can't solely rely on the skill-based methodologies to dictate what is important in life, nor can we allow it to measure or define who we are. We are more than the sum of our skills.

I recently went on several skill-and evidence-based model websites to look at their curriculum. The largest areas of skills these approaches address are: Behavior, Communication, Self- Help, and Living Skills. If we add up all of these skills, do they provide us with well-rounded, thoughtful and loving children? Put simply, if you want to teach your child a skill quickly, use a skill-based approach. However, if you want to teach your child how to be a become a participating, caring, loving, conscientious adult, and how to live a life worth living, my suggestion is that you choose a socially-based approach like The Social Diet→. One is *not better* than the other. They serve completely different functions, and I think we need both in order to best serve our children.

I can use my love of French as an example of the necessity of using an immersion approach, coupled with a skill-based approach. I went to France for the first time when I was 9 years old, and fell in love with it. After I came back, I wanted to become fluent in the language and someday even study there and become a French teacher (which I did). After that first summer, I went back to France practically every year. I was addicted. My French became almost perfect, to the point where a French person thought I was French (one of my biggest compliments, at the time). The point here is that I learned French *both* from being immersed in it each summer when I was in the country engaging with the native French people, and having real time experiences, but I also learned French back in the U.S. in my classrooms which were not authentic. I read as much as I could, and I studied as hard as I could. I was motivated to study grammar books and poetry. I learned faster and better because I used an immersion approach, but it was coupled with a more traditional direct approach. It was only both together which allowed me to excel at the language faster than I could have using only one approach. So, you see, immersion was great, but so was more methodical learning. I think I needed both to be as well rounded and well prepared for attending school in France as a graduate student.

That being said, I admit that I am biased: I did enjoy my time in France more than sitting in a classroom, or my bedroom, studying the language. In other words, children who struggle the most socially should receive an intervention which allows him/her to spend most of the day interacting in community. This is truly what The Social Diet is all about—spending most of the day immersed with real people, in real ways, in rich stimulating environments, with the help of qualified practitioners who are able to sustain the engagement and make it motivating, fun and educational. This kind of socially enhanced curriculum should be practiced until the child has the basics in their ability to relate to people. The social and emotional piece is our foundation. I do think family, relationships, and social connectedness are the more important things in life than accumulating skills.

I believe in the 80/20 rule: Eighty percent of a child's curriculum should be spent in authentic face-to-face interactions in ways that support their well-being- the social emotional milestones needed for a successful, purposeful life in adulthood. At least until the child has the basics in their ability to relate to people. The other 20 percent of our children's time must be spent learning skills and information that will help support them in task-oriented situations (those that require tangible steps from a beginning to a specific end-point.) In this 20 percent, the human factor isn't considered or needed-- task-oriented thinking is. Both are necessary in life, but each has a different focus, and each serves our children.

We need to nurture and feed the human piece first. What this means at 80 percent of your child's time is that your child would receive an intervention which allows him/her to spend most of the day immersed in community. This is truly what The Social Diet is all about-- spending most of the day interacting with real people, in real ways, in rich, stimulating environments, with the help of qualified practitioners who are able to sustain the engagement and make it motivating, fun, and educational. Children have only so much brain power, and they can learn skills at any age. Child Development experts, however, tell us that learning what it means to be and act human is best learned at an early age before the brain is asked to perform specific functions. The stronger and more stable the social and emotional foundation are in children, (neurotypical or non-neurotypical), the higher chance they have at becoming thinking, social/emotional beings, and the more success they will have in having a fulfilling, happy life.

As in all lives, our children's skills should reflect who they are as individuals. We know that our experiences in life are what tell us what skills we need, not the reverse. Wouldn't it be better for children to get to choose what they want based on allowing them to have rich experiences which feed their human side, rather than to guess or presuppose where and how they should be spending their time in adulthood? What each of us is drawn to naturally is the best predictor of who we become as adults. Every one of us has the right to choose our own path. Our internal "beingness," and our connection to a culture where we have societal responsibility, is what drives our external contributions and gifts. Let us not deny our children this human privilege.

We can't be expected to simply learn a set of skills and think they are enough to become all that we are meant to be in this world. We cannot become social beings simply from learning skills. Instead, we can only become connected, social beings by spending endless hours actually being with other human beings in meaningful, engaged, and authentic ways. This must be the goal we also have for our children, those neurotypical as well as non-neurotypical. The current culture of autism, though, is focused on a hard-skills model, often at the expense of working on the *relating* skills that our children on the spectrum most definitely need in their daily diet.

With this kind of mentality and practice, we may be robbing our children of their most precious gift—their humanness.

Cultural Assumption Number 3:

Reward-based Systems Work

The field of Behavior Modification is predicated upon the belief that behavior can be changed if we reinforce the positive behaviors, and extinguish the poor behaviors. We, as a society, think that rewards and punishments work well as a way to change behavior. Take "Johnny" for example.

Johnny has learned that if he wants dessert (the added, positive reinforcement), he needs to eat most of his dinner. If he doesn't eat most of his dinner (the undesired behavior) he will not get dessert (the imposed consequence). We have all had this sort of experience: Do something "good" and we get what we want. Do something bad and we don't. Parents (myself included) have used rewards and punishments for as long as we have had children (as have teachers and other professionals who work with children). I am not disputing the value of positive (adding in) or negative (taking away) reinforcements in societies and families. However, this "truth" may be camouflaging other truths that may be limiting us and our children.

Research, and my own experiences, have shown me that reward systems do not work long term, over years and decades. While they might work initially, and you may quickly see the results that you hope to experience for your child, research shows that positive or negative reinforcement does not affect long-term changes in behavior.[6] In fact, there is a very large body of research that shows that the use of rewards and punishment can even be detrimental, if overused. This, of course, seems counterintuitive. However, the use of rewards and punishment teaches children (all children, not just special needs children) that their behavior is controlled by *outside* influences. Without realizing it perhaps, children are being *conditioned* to act a certain way because they have learned that they will either get something good or bad in return. They do it for the reward of having something they want, or to avoid something they don't.

What is wrong with the above scenario? On the surface, *nothing*. When we evaluate this cultural assumption, we, the adults, may be conditioned ourselves to think that this is all we can expect from our child. We assume that we cannot expect that children—especially children with autism— will be able to choose the right behavior for intrinsic purposes. We expect immediate behavioral change, not the emotional and neurological changes, which then enhance permanent behavioral change.

I believe that we have been conditioned not to *expect* anything else. If we don't expect it, our children will only rise to our low

---

[6] Kohn, Alfie. (1999). *Punished by Rewards.* New York: Houghton Mifflin Co. McCullers, John C. (1978). In Pepper, Mark R. and Greene, David, *The Hidden Costs of Rewards: New Perspectives on the Psychology of Human Motivation.* Hillsdale, N.J.: Erlbaum.

expectations. I see this all the time with my clients' families and at their schools. The bar or standard is preset, and it is low. We learn to believe that the only way our child can learn is through extrinsic (external) reinforcement. The irony here is that with this kind of conditioning, we are reinforcing a narrowed vision of our children's potential. Very few of us, as parents, have this as our goal, for ourselves or for our children.

Children are very clever. If we are not careful, they will condition *us* to get what they want and the reinforcements they demand can get out of control. One example comes to mind. A mother told me that she had to "bribe" her 12-year-old daughter with an exorbitant amount of money so she would come to see me. The sad part is that the mother didn't think there was anything wrong with this. She had been so accustomed to having to reward her child for the littlest things that by the time she was 12, she had her mother twisted around her little finger. This is, of course, not a healthy situation. Over time, both mother and daughter learned that they had to reward a behavior that should not have ever required a reward. I wondered what this child would demand when she was 15? 21? Reward systems may work for parents to get a desired behavior in the short term, but by reinforcing these behaviors, they just might create other problems.

There is a great deal of good to be said for learning to make the right choices based on moral, social, and cognitive values.

How are children ever going to learn how to do the right thing when they become adults, if we don't teach them how to problem-solve and think for themselves? How will our children ever know how to behave with others, show empathy, and learn how to be good, responsible people if they are more concerned about what is in it for them? The great gift we can give our children is our own realization that they can learn how to make right choices. They can learn that being a good person matters and they can learn to want to do the right thing.

This concept definitely applies to children with autism, although it's most commonly used in parenting styles for neurotypical children. If our special needs children are given the kind of instruction that fosters "doing the right thing because it is the right thing to do" they can learn this is necessary, not just for assimilation into society norms, but to live a happy and fulfilling life. I have seen this happen with many children whose families instill this way of thinking into their daily practices. I understand that not every child will be able to act responsibly, or be fully independent, but in my experience, most can, even the ones with significant autism *if and only if* that is what adults expect from them on a consistent basis. One thing is certain—if we don't think our children can do better, they will not.

This is not about causing your child to be perceived as "normal." This is about their lives being happy, fulfilling, and beneficial to themselves and to society.

Consider this: When people learn to act a certain way according to what they think others want, they can never become authentic. There is no sense of self that is established. There is a sense that we do things according to others' rules. Children and adults who follow this teaching pattern learn that their behavior is conditional upon their performance and, depending on that performance, either good or bad things happen.

Cultural Assumption Number 4:

People with Autism Can't….

The culture of autism wants to make us believe that our children on the spectrum *can't* do "x, y, and z." So many times, I hear blanket statements, such as, "Kids with autism can't generalize." "Kids with autism struggle at school." "They can't make friends." "They act out, and their behaviors are poor."

It may be true that our children with social cognitive delays face harder challenges than the average child, but we want to be careful not to allow what we *hear* to become our *truth*. We, as humans, have the propensity to believe what we hear, especially if we hear it repeated enough times, we typically accept it as fact or as a given. This can be self-defeating, since, before we realize it, we may be making decisions which could be perpetuating our children's limitations. The fact of the matter is: *If you think they can't, they will prove you right each time. If you think they can and insist they can, they will also prove you right each time!*

I know this from personal experience with my own son. If I didn't think Ylann could learn to think about other people, to be kind and demonstrate empathy, he would not be the caring person he is today.

Moreover, if I had convinced myself that my son could not learn how to behave appropriately, he would probably still be exhibiting the kinds of major meltdowns he did at the age of 2. The behaviors would just probably be more severe, since we didn't address them earlier, and since his feelings and body are much larger. If I did not expect him to be able to make friends, he probably would not have any, but he does. If I didn't expect that he would be able to navigate middle school with 750 other kids, he wouldn't-- but he did, completely on his own. If I didn't think he could handle mainstream education as a young child, he would not have been able to be in all regular classes as he is now and do it brilliantly with no additional support.

Ylann is able to achieve all these things not because he necessarily wanted to push himself. In fact quite the opposite is true-- he still hates to push himself and I still have to make sure he is pushed. He also was not able to achieve all this because I got lucky and had a son who was "high-functioning." He was (and still is) able to achieve amazing things for himself because he has a parent who expects that he can! If I, his own mother, did *not* believe that Ylann could learn "x, y, and z", I am positive that he would be a completely different person than he is today. I made sure that everyone who worked with Ylann adopt the determined, empowered mindset that "Yes, he can!" and not allow for anything less.

I realize, though, that this is daunting, especially with your own expectations changed by your child's diagnosis, and the professionals whom you have consulted. Do not let your child's diagnosis or delays define who they are. This is your child who happens to have certain challenges, like everyone else in life. Don't make the mistake of listening to what the culture might be reinforcing or telling you how you should think. There is a very powerful distinction to be made here that I ask you to think about, because it alone can determine your child's future potential: your child's diagnosis is not *them*. That is not who they are. A diagnosis may contribute to your understanding of why they *behave* the way they do, but even that does not mean they can't learn how to behave and exist differently in the world.

This point is so important that I want to give you another example of how this works. Let's take a child who is 6 years old and has autism. His behaviors have become very challenging. He has tantrums at home, and at school. He shouts, he kicks, he hits. He refuses to do seemingly simple things, like sit at the table during mealtime, or sit at his desk as the other kids at school do. This is stressful enough, but is only a fraction of what he does each day. His behaviors according to Mom and Dad are only getting worse.

You might recognize your own child here. This child's behaviors are not out of the ordinary for children with developmental delays. In fact, they are *so ordinary* that we as a culture have come to the cultural assumption that has come to *expect* this kind of behavior. After all, "Poor 'Timothy' has autism, he *can't* be expected to know how to behave."

Actually, yes, he can! Not only can he be expected to behave, but he needs desperately for us (the adults in his life) to expect him to do so. Having the cultural assumption that he *can't* will perpetuate the problem behavior. What I am saying here is a fundamental truth in human nature: *What we expect or don't expect is what shows up in life for us.* As the adults in our children's lives, we have the responsibility to truly understand this ideal, and change our expectations…not to lower them to what we are told to expect, nor punish for not exceeding what is needed, but to find balance and ever increasing goals for our children.

Pushing through the "Cant's" is not an easy task. Believe me, it would have been much easier for me to follow the cultural expectation. The thinking would have been, "Oh, that's too hard for him, he doesn't like that, he can't do that." With this idea comes the unspoken implication, "…so let's not even try."

Even though my son and my clients sometimes exhaust me, I do not allow myself or them to give up. I refuse to give up because the alternative is *not* doing what is needed for our kids to reach their true potential. It has been proven to me that our children can do almost anything and everything we think is possible.

Questions to Consider:

- How are we looking at our children with disabilities?
- Are we able to see past the disability?
- If we are really honest with ourselves, might we be able to catch ourselves (albeit unconsciously at first) setting lower expectations because our cultural assumption has made us believe that our children "Can't?"

- Are there predetermined assumptions, notions *or* practices that may be getting in the way of your child's growth? What are they?

Cultural Assumption Number 5:

If We Change Challenging Behaviors, We Have Reached Our Goal

This cultural assumption, I have found, goes something like this: "If we take care of the *behaviors,* there is no more treatment necessary." Many parents and professionals espouse this way of thinking without even realizing it. I want to emphasize that eliminating problem behaviors are an important piece of the puzzle, but solving this piece is only the start of intervention and should not be the finish line. This is something the current culture of autism fails to understand. All kids with autism struggle with challenging behaviors. Behavioral problems are so widespread and such an important topic that it is probably the most talked about and written about area for our children on the spectrum. I, too, write about it (see the next chapter), but I believe that we need an intervention model that includes looking beyond challenging behaviors.

Moreover, if we look at this issue from a cultural perspective, we might be able to see that we are selling ourselves and our children short. When I examine what is actually happening with my clients, I would venture that more than 90 percent of their days at school, therapy or elsewhere is spent on adults trying to get them to behave or be compliant. The conventional thinking at school is this: once they get the behaviors under control, the child (and therapist) has done their job. Under this formulaic approach, once children no longer have major behavioral problems, they are perceived as no longer needing any more support. I witness this fallacy practically every day! Unfortunately, this equation style learning pattern is simply insufficient. Ylann could never have written a letter to me like he did, if all I cared about were his behaviors. Focusing only on behaviors is a huge oversight on our part because it takes a myopic view of what our children need. Behavioral compliance should only be the *first* step in our interventions. Good behavior is a prerequisite for success, including in The Social Diet, but we need a standard intervention model for autism that goes well beyond behavioral concerns. The current treatment mandated by our present culture of autism is only partially successful as it only goes so far. We need a model that will prepare children for real life that includes social and emotional well-being.

School is Not Enough

I know that schools truly believe that they prepare our children for life, but in the last 15 years in the field, I think I can count only a handful of schools that do the full extent of this important work. To no fault of their own, school staff are overworked, underpaid, and underfunded in the best instances, and especially when it comes to special needs children, public school intervention is not enough, in and of itself. You cannot count on the schools to do all of the teaching for your child. They don't have the training, or even funding for training, which they need. Secondly, they are mandated by the state to teach the academic curriculum, which may or may not be possible for all neurological profiles in the special needs sector. Even if they wanted to take more time for the social piece, they are not set up for establishing it. Also, there is not enough time at school which is devoted to social integration in order to make the difference that our kids need. You, the parent, must supplement the school curriculum if you want to give your child the social piece, and if you want to follow The Social Diet.

It is not the school's job to teach your child how to behave. That is the job of the parents at home. It is not fair or logical to expect that a teacher can set limits and boundaries, if they are not set up and adhered to at home. I know that we parents are stressed, and we have too much on our plates. But, when it comes to teaching your child what is acceptable and not acceptable behavior, you have got to take this on. If you do not, everyone loses. Your child will have a miserable time at school because most of his school day will be teachers having to take on the role of police. The teachers also lose out, because instead of your child being there for learning, he is not yet ready to learn. You can't learn anything if you are not regulated, meaning that you cannot attend to what is going on in your environment in an appropriate manner. Please do not blame the school about your child's behavior if you yourself haven't trained them first. Again, while it does take a village, a teacher or staff member can team up and reinforce what you have done at home, but they can not replace you and your responsibilities. I devote an entire chapter on setting boundaries and limits. It is a prerequisite for The Social Diet and a prerequisite for participating in social arenas including school.

The Disconnect

As a Sociolinguist, it is my job to listen to what people say, what people believe, and what they value. When I ask parents what they want for their children when they are adults, I get the same kinds of answers. "I want my child to be happy; I want my child to have friends; I want my child to get married, have children, and have a good job." When I ask parents, who have kids with autism the same question, the answers are practically identical, except there is more urgency for the parents to want their child to fit in, have friends, and be accepted. It became quite clear that there is a gaping disconnect between the end goal of living a loving, socially-connected life with meaning, and the practically non-existent curriculum to get our children to that goal. We say we want our kids to be happy, find love, become parents, and have wonderful experiences that help mold them. Yet, there is nothing in place at school, where they spend the majority of their daily hours, which teaches them how to accomplish this exceptionally difficult task. Even when our kids are at home, parents are so busy just getting through their day, and their kids come home tired and have to do homework and sports. When are they supposed to learn the human life skills to be in healthy relationships, which lead to healthy lifestyles? Into this normal complication to family life, then add the difficulties of learning social communication as if it is a foreign language, and the added exhaustion to the body and emotions which comes with living a non-neurotypical life in a predominantly neurotypical society. We say that a life worth living is one that is based in love and caring. How are we going to find love and balance when we live in a culture that doesn't support that? I have to say, from the perspective of someone who studies the behavior of human beings, this common practice, rooted in business, is madness.

Ask any parent of a child with autism, and I can guarantee that they are not satisfied with their child's ability to know how to relate with others. This is the average parents' number one concern. I get most of my calls from mothers who are dying inside because their child doesn't know how to develop relationships. They tell me their child has no real friends. At school they are typically found by themselves at lunch, recess, and without a partner at gym. At home, they are not asked out for play dates or to attend parties. For the lucky few who are, most often they do not act appropriately, in the visiting parent's expectations, at least not enough to be asked to visit a second time. This ongoing worry leaves parents feeling helpless. How can their child learn how to be in the world?

I believe we are focusing on the wrong things and therefore are not getting the results we want.

Focus on What's Important

Inevitably, a parent is worried that her child can't "do" any number of things, coupled with their worries of their child not having friends. The list of worries seems endless. "My child still isn't toilet trained. My child won't listen or eat healthy foods. My child is struggling at school, and doesn't know how to read, do math, or write."

You name it, I've heard it, and they are all valid concerns. However, what do we need to tackle first? Should we focus on the hard skills that can be learned at any age, or should we learn the life skills we need to live a connected, more loving, more meaningful life first?

It would be wonderful if we could do both, but often our children do not have the mental bandwidth for learning both essentials at the same time. If you overload that bandwidth before it is given a chance to expand, I believe you are setting up both you and your child for failure.

In life there is only so much time. We cannot do everything; we have to make choices. When you have a child with a developmental delay or social challenges, this is even more critical. Recently, I witnessed a Speech Pathologist having a speech session with a 4-year-old boy on the spectrum. For 60 minutes the boy was to sit still in his chair at the table and learn to point with one finger, one time, to the object the therapist or parent indicated. When I asked them what the goal of the session was, she replied "To get Tommy to point once and only once at his device." I sat there, my heart dying. This child had so many social, emotional and behavioral needs, and this is how the professionals are having him spend his time? For one full hour, learning how to point one time to a picture on his communication device? To what end, for what purpose? Is this really how we want our 4-year-olds to be spending their time and energy, a child who could not yet relate to another human being? Although the professionals were well intentioned, this child lost out on any real meaningful learning.

What do we need to do to help our children be more successful?

I have come to love and revere The Social Diet. I have cultivated and nursed it. I have laughed with it, cried through it, and been through a challenging personal and professional journey to bring it to the light of day. I don't know if the nation is ready to embrace a culture that puts more value on people on our relationships and quality of life than we do on what we "produce." We are taught, even as young toddlers, that we must conform, in order to fit in and be accepted. We are rewarded for what we do rather than who we are. We live in a culture where we are not able to be free to be ourselves, to live with open hearts, and lead lives of simple peace and joy. We are taught to be hyper-vigilant and to make sure we have the external commodities that deem us likable, lovable, and worthy. We live in a culture where the external façade is deemed more important than our internal needs.

What I like so much about the autism community is that we all *have to be real.* It doesn't matter if we make a lot of money, or if we live on food stamps. If you have a child with ASD or related delays, you are exposed in the national culture, often to scorn, or the assumption that your parenting is at fault. All of our facades become stripped away, leaving each of us exposed in our deeply interesting, deeply flawed humanity. However, I think this is the silver lining. We get to become very real-- which means not perfect. We get to be vulnerable and become better people because of our children's challenges. We get to witness our children's struggles, acknowledge our own, and see that of those around us. In fact, I think we are the ones who have a shot at turning our culture around. We have the clearest picture of what's really important in life and what isn't, because when you have a special needs child, the things which are not important in life get stripped away, leaving only the most critical and necessary things.

This demands a new way of *living.* It will stop our American culture in its incessant need to be "number one." This entails giving up our engrained competitive side to be the best, fastest, strongest, or biggest. It requires us to slow down and breathe in order to attend to what matters most to us- our family and our community. It will expose our flaws, if we have not lived according to our values, and teaches us to change our minds and hearts to point towards what must matter. It requires us to redefine who we are as a people, and as a nation, and set different priorities for our society and culture. I think it's time to make this happen, and it is very possible.

The Social Diet is designed to teach you the unequivocal importance of prioritizing your life, so your child can go as far as humanly possible. It is designed to give you the tools that you will need as a parent to model a balanced, healthy and connected, meaningful life, so that you can pass this on to your children. It invites you to take your productivity mask down because it does not support you. It invites you to roll up your sleeves and feel the emotions you have when the mask is down and heal that grief. Then it will engage you in an education of how you can help your child connect with himself and others. These are the parents who will be successful at teaching their children The Social Diet. They will be successful because they, too, have learned how to put relationships and their family's well-being first.

The Social Diet is not for the meek or weary, but you are neither of those things, because you want what is best for your child, and are willing to research to find what works for your family. It is, however, for people who are willing to do the hard work, who are not afraid to face themselves and their current lifestyle, make the changes that need to be made to put their child's needs ahead of their own. The rewards that you will find when choosing to live The Social Diet way are immense and will open your heart and allow you to connect to your child in ways you may not have thought ever possible. Having a special needs child will change you, but I want you to know this: you get to choose how you change. You choose how these things bless and shape your life. Hopefully, The Social Diet will be one of those tools which instigates healthy changes for your family.

Redefining Autism- A New Working Definition

In the chapters that follow, I propose a significant paradigm shift- one that moves away from "skill building" and moves toward a more "relationship-based" model. For it is *through* relationships **that all children** learn how to connect with others and think for themselves. This ultimately will allow our children a better chance at dealing with life and living it to its fullest.

Treat the Autism, Not the Symptoms of Autism.

In my opinion, the paradigm shift needs to start with a broader understanding of what autism is. As a field, we seem to be treating autism based on its symptoms, rather than treating the underlining cause. This awareness alone can benefit us enormously. If we stop focusing on the symptoms alone, we stand a better chance at tackling the cause head on. In this chapter I invite you to adopt a new definition of autism--one that will enable us to readjust and rethink our current perspective.

I thought I understood what Autism was when I first started out in the field. I, too, was encultured to think of autism in a certain way. Then, as part of my Relationship Development Intervention® training, I learned the true definition of autism, which would change the way I thought about it and the way I went about treating it and helping families. What I learned during my first day of training was profound.

I can recall our trainer writing the following phrase on the white board:

True or false: *"Autism is a behavioral, language, social and sensory disorder?"*

"Of course, that is true. Everybody knows that!" When I learned it was *false*, I was shocked and confused. How could it *not* be true? What else could autism be? I did not have the answer, but my instructor did. The light bulb went off and my passion and appreciation for autism was born. The trainer went on to explain, "If we replace the word "is" with the word "affects," then the above statement would be a true."

What I learned that day is that Autism *affects* behavior, it *affects* language, it *affects* social relations and the sensory system. Autism affects just about everything in one's life, but, that is not what Autism *is.* Poor behaviors, language problems, poor social skills, and a dysregulated sensory system are all *symptoms* of the disorder, but they do not explain what autism is at its core.

Suddenly it struck me-- if we, as parents and professionals, want to treat people with autism, we need to make sure we are treating the *autism* and not only the *symptoms* of autism.

I learned from my training that when a person has autism, it means that they do not process information the same way a more neurotypical brain would. Humans are processing information every millisecond of each day. By *processing information,* I mean that we take in information from all of our senses, and all of that information gets processed into the brain. The processing of such information allows us to make sense of our world. Our brains tells us what information is important, specifically what we need to pay attention to (for example the smell of dinner burning) and what we can let go (the sound of the neighbor mowing his lawn). Our brains also tell us how to regulate our emotions and how to organize or plan out our thinking. In essence, when the brain is able to function normally, or within a normal range, we are able to act and react to the stimulus normally, and ignore unimportant stimuli.

Knowing how to make sense or process the information our senses take in is even more critical today than ever before. More than ever before in history, our poor brains are being bombarded with information, faster than we can blink an eye. With the current environment, it is unavoidable to go into sensory overload, given the number of things begging for our attention in the world. It's amazing that *any one* of us can make sense of our environment.

Now, imagine that you have Autism, and your brain is not able to do this processing very well. This means that a brain with autism doesn't take in and process sensory information the same way a "normal" brain does. With autism, the different processing centers of the brain are not working efficiently. This can have devastating effects for how this population perceives and interacts in the social world.

The brain is essentially an electrical system, where brain cells, neurons, are specifically designed to conduct electrical signals. These electrical signals, impulses, travel down the axons to branches or dendrites, where they are then able to jump and enter the branches of neighboring neurons. Basically, this is like cars being on a superhighway, traveling at high speeds down interstates and local highways. They want to get to their destinations as quickly and efficiently as possible, by the shortest, best route.

For a person with autism, their neurons have gone awry. The neurotransmitters, which are chemicals in the brain that we rely on to communicate with the brain's different parts, are malfunctioning. These neurotransmitters are not efficiently sending messages between the brain and the body. In other words, the brain may or may not be taking in and processing the information it needs to act and react in a normal fashion. This happens in many different disorders to different degrees. Depression, bipolar disorders, ADHD, all involve neurotransmitters either moving too quickly, too slowly, or not going where they are supposed to go. It's a very common problem, but it works slightly differently in the case of Autism.

To continue our superhighway metaphor, a "normally" functioning brain is able to use the "superhighway" when different parts of information from the brain need to commute (or communicate) to other parts of the brain. The brain can quickly figure out what it needs to do, and feel, in any number of situations- expected or unexpected. Most people's brains are able to drive on the super highway without a problem- they know where to go and proceed naturally. Their reaction time is good, regardless of whether a dog runs in front of their car, or they need to get off at a particular exit. They rarely get lost, and have a good GPS system for navigating through difficulties.

If you have an autistic brain however, instead of being able to take the superhighway where your brain-car is zooming along properly, your brain forces you to take the back country "off-roads." This detour route can be full of dead ends, or jerky starts and stops, which can leave the person confused and not sure how to act or feel, especially in unexpected situations. This is where you see the symptoms of autism coming out; they are the direct result of someone whose brain is not able to account for, and make sense of, the kind of information that is a being presented to him. He is unable to process his world accurately.

"Use it or lose it": Why seeing Autism as a processing disorder is so critical

One of the biggest problems for people who have autism is that they have a static way of thinking. If you have a brain that does not process very well, you will probably want things in your life to be repetitive, reliable, replicable, stable, predictable, rule driven. That would make total sense! If something worked for you yesterday, you will expect that it will work for you today. What is so bad about static? We all like and need static, actually. Aren't you glad that a red light always means stop and that a green light always means go? Do we not rely on schedules and set routines? Of course, we do. We all need static in our lives. It gives us order.

But, real life is never static; it is constantly changing. It is not predictable, and sometimes events are beyond our control. If we are not able to adapt to the changes that unfold, life can be very challenging. For people with autism, this can be very tricky. The inability to shift gears when necessary can put a person with autism into a complete meltdown. We call this dysregulation.

I do not think that keeping their lives static is the answer our children need. Quite the contrary, in fact. If we, the adults, try to keep things the same for our children with autism, I think we are doing them quite a disservice. I believe that our ultimate job is to teach our children how to make sense of their environment. Essentially, I believe it is our job to be their guides, to help them process incoming information, and give them the tools they will need to navigate the naturally ever-changing world.

The brain has a "Use it or lose it" capability. As with any muscle, it learns through exercise and practice. The kind of exercise and practice it gains is critical for different types of outcomes. Give the brain a steady diet of repetitive tasks, and it will become proficient with these tasks. It runs the risk, however, of becoming more and more rigid as the brain gets used to doing only the same repetitive actions. Over time, the brain comes to expect this kind of stimulus and will not do well if we challenge it, or change things up.

Give the brain a diet of supported novel experiences, however, and it will learn to adapt, and even grow accustomed to receiving new challenges. This is the direction in which I think we need go when treating those with autism.

Creating a Paradigm Shift: Moving away from a Skill-Based Instruction to Socially-Based Learning

Our current *culture of autism* reinforces a rote skill-based instruction approach.

I am proposing that we make a shift away from the typical repetitive skill-based instruction to more socially or relationship-based model. We will talk more about that in the next chapters.

My job as both a Sociolinguist and a Mom is to inform people (parents in this case) to be discriminatory consumers. Our kids are too important to let others tell you what to do. Autism is a very emotional provoking disorder. Most of us are shell-shocked when we get the news. We don't know what to do or where to go or who to trust. We do tend to latch on to what other professionals are saying especially when you hear it being repeated by others. But please, do not let the culture of anything dictate what you should or should not be doing. This is a personal choice. Your best ally is to arm yourself with education rather than jumping into treatment services. It is imperative when you're picking an approach for your child, especially when it comes to something as significant as Autism Spectrum Disorder and the like, that you have done your own research and spoken to a variety of people who bring other gifts to the table. You also want to talk to parents who have used alternative methods and see what the outcomes have looked like.

To me, it is impossible to envision a methodology out there that does not take our human factor as its foundation, but most do not. I tell people all the time, "It doesn't take a Ph.D. to understand that if (in this particular case) we want to teach our children how to be social, how to connect on a human level, we need a Social approach." Years later, I realize, maybe it does take a Ph.D. to point this out. So, it is an honor to allow me to do this for my readers.

We must never forget that no matter what we do in life, no matter where we go, or what we need to learn, we are first and foremost a social being. If we fail to nurture that, if we spend most of our awake hours whether it be at home, school, work or wherever, if this place is devoid of feeding our soul and our passion and without a human connection, we are headed, in my opinion, for a life with little meaning or fulfillment.

Chapter Reflection Questions:

- Is the use of rewards and punishment the only way for our children with autism to learn how to behave?
- Are you limiting your child's potential from espousing this sole viewpoint?
- How might you be limiting your own mindset with this way of thinking?
- Could you imagine another possibility? Could your child learn to act in a certain way?

Please take a moment and list your preconceived ideas — what do you believe your child will NEVER accomplish?

Once you have completed your list, write another list stating the exact opposite making it become a new possibility. Use an affirmative communication style to declare this. For example, if you think that your child "can't make friends" I want you to write down, "My child can make friends and he will make friends."

What have you noticed happens when you change a negative mindset into a positive one?

• CHAPTER 4 •

What The Social Diet® Is

It is important for parents to be able to create a social immersion approach for real-life learning for their children, and The Social Diet is the technique that will help get them to that goal. Real-life learning, according to The Social Diet, is one that goes beyond self. It is a life which is grounded in teaching *values,* anchored with a strong *moral code* which is based in respect for all. This is an approach which comes from the heart. If implemented correctly, it will give you the tools that you and your family need to live together in harmony and peace. At the same time, it will open new ways of thinking about your lifestyle and how you want to live. It will teach you how to slow down, prioritize what is really important to your values and beliefs, and give you permission to make those things your top priority while raising your children. In a world which is out of balance, The Social Diet allows you to reclaim your life in a way that feeds and nourishes you and those you love the most—your family.

7 Practical Ways The Social Diet Will Help Your Family

The Social Diet is:

1) For families who yearn to have a deeper connection with their children, but do not necessarily know how to do that or even know where to start.
2) To help parents learn how to parent children who are struggling socially. These children may have, or exhibit signs of Autism Spectrum Disorder (ASD), Asperger's, ADD/ADHD, or any social or cognitive developmental delay.
3) To help parents prioritize and think about the bigger picture. Your children may be 2 or 4 years old, or even 12, but they will be adults far longer than they will be children. You want to make sure that what you are doing today will be helpful for your children in the future.
4) To remind parents to have the very highest of expectations, and to never to give up hope, while celebrating each triumph.
5) To give parents the tools they need to be successful teachers and communicator advocates on behalf of their children.
6) To give parents the strength and courage they need to navigate this complex and confusing journey of parenting a non-neurotypical child.
7) To investigate our role as a society, and what we can do to make sure that our basic human needs and the needs of our children are being met. More specifically, to understand the

social-emotional needs of every human being, so that together you and your children do not just survive but can actually *thrive*.

The Philosophy of The Social Diet→

The Social Diet is, like all diets and lifestyle changes, both a philosophy and way of life. Both understanding the concept and reasons for a change, and creating the change are equality important. We must first understand the *why* before we can practice the *doing*.

The Social Diet is a gift we give ourselves, which allows you to connect with your child in ways you may never have dreamt possible. It is a gift in the sense that you get to choose what you want for your life and the lives of your children, which gives you the right and ability to create your own vision. It is a gift of empowerment which can give you the courage to *not* allow others to influence your decisions about how you *should* think what you *should* do for your family, and gives you permission to say, "No, I prefer to do *x, y, & z,* instead, thank you." It is a gift which gives you a voice that says "I matter, my child matters," and which educates you to appreciate the miraculous little things that happen every day which can sometimes go unnoticed. It is a gift which allows you, the parent, to have the honor of being the best kind of parent you can be. It is a gift of respect for yourself and for your child, and one of respect which your child has for you and others. It is a gift that gives back joy, laughter, and tears at any given moment of any given day.

Finally, The Social Diet is a gift of love-- the love which we have for ourselves, our children and our world.

The Social Diet→ is a Way of Living

Typically, we associate a *diet* as having to do with food. People "go on a diet," which means they want to lose weight by decreasing their food intake. I use the term *diet* in almost the opposite way. Instead of a diet being associated with loss or less, I want use the word as it was originally intended.

The origin of the word *diet* comes from Latin *dieta* and Greek *diatia,* meaning *way of living*. The Social Diet is a conscious way of living. As such, it is a *daily practice* that parents choose to adopt. Through continuous daily *practice* we learn how to embrace the kind of thinking and behaving that is necessary to produce the outcomes we want to see in our lives. When we do this practice, over time, it becomes *a diet for daily living*. My goal is that through daily practices you will learn how to regain control of how you *think,* and *behave*. You will learn how your behavior impacts your child's way of behaving.

The Social Diet deliberately sets the foundation for you to make *proactive,* conscious decisions rather than *reactive* ones. The goal is not to be putting out fires every day, but to be able to live for a higher, more impactful purpose, and to set the tone for a more deliberate lifestyle. The Social Diet encourages you as a parent to engage in deep meaningful relationships with your children as your first priority. The teaching of superficial or rote task-oriented learning is secondary, and even discouraged, for young children who lag behind socially.

What The Social Diet is Not

The Social Diet is not a recipe or an approach that children can memorize. It is alive and fluid, much like your life is. Can you memorize how it is that you behave, think, and relate to others? Certainly not, and neither can your children. This is not a curriculum which can be memorized or learned as a quick fix to your child's problem behaviors or social challenges, because behavior issues and social challenges do not occur overnight, and neither will the solutions. So, The Social Diet may require a lifestyle changes that will take some time to see improvements, but the improvements can be lifelong and will be worth every minute you spend on the program.

Not Just "Social Skills"

The Social Diet does not mean learning "social skills" in the traditional way. In our culture, social skills are generally taught in an artificial environment (classroom or office), and the curriculum is usually scripted or predetermined. This kind of curriculum functions to prepare the child for what to do or say in specific social situations. Although this can be helpful at times, this way of learning frequently translates into children failing to learn how to behave, communicate, and think in real-world situations which are not scripted or predictable. As such we need the ability to be able to think for ourselves and act on whatever comes our way. This kind of life preparation can only be learned through real time, genuine *social interactions*.

Not Just Traditional Classrooms with Typical Peers

The Social Diet is also *not* simply placing your child with special needs next to their neurotypical peers. Unless your child's therapy program is developmentally appropriate, has the right kind of adult support, and is provided the specific kinds of experiences which are needed for this kind of growth and development, your child may not be benefiting from their neurotypical peers as much as you hope.

This may seem like a contradiction of my total immersion approach. My caveat is that researchers have found that people, including children, do best in immersion environments when they are *developmentally ready*. For example, let's say you want to learn Chinese, but you are a novice. The experts have found that having at least a rudimentary background in the language before you arrive in China is beneficial to your further developing proficient language skills. It has been shown that the greatest gains are made with people who are *ready* to take advantage of being in the native country, and, of course, this makes sense. If you didn't speak a word of Chinese and were dropped in China, you would struggle immensely, and be concerned about embarrassing mistakes and cultural mishaps. But, let's say you had already studied the basics of Chinese, the phonemic (sounds), grammatical structures, and the way of life (rituals, traditions, etc.). You will learn more quickly and go further than a novice speaker who spends the same amount of time there.

It amazes me how many parents, and even professionals, believe that placing non-neurotypical (non-NT) children with neurotypical (NT) peers will miraculously result in non-NT children being socialized adequately for their needs. I wish it were that simple…but it's not. If we take a child with autism, for example, and place him in a mainstream classroom, the benefits may not be as great as you might expect. A lot depends on the child's developmental readiness to learn from others. Even for those children who are developmentally ready or "higher functioning," having typical classmates will still not be sufficient to learn the complex underpinnings of what it means to be a social being. If it were that simple (putting autistic children with neurotypical kids) we would no longer have autism. Without intention, awareness and specific kinds of interactions with native speakers, one cannot simply "pick up" how to be social. It takes a lot of work, education, guidance, and many years of practice.

Therefore, placing our children with autism or autistic-like behavior together with neurotypical kids does not mean that the child is being socialized, nor does it necessarily provide the environment this child needs for real-world learning. Yes, it is probably better than isolation, but without providing a steady diet of authentic, developmentally appropriate *partnered social interactions*, a child may make little progress.

And, progress, of course, is what we all desire for our children.

Partnering up in The Social Diet®: The Senior and Junior Partnership

The Social Diet→ is a daily practice that you and your children do *together*. It occurs in real time, in real situations throughout the day. Building partnerships is one of the seven most important ingredients for The Social Diet. The parent or primary caregiver plays the role of the senior partner, and the child is given the role of the junior partner. You cannot participate in The Social Diet if you are not with your junior partner. Your partnership with your child is the vehicle through which the child becomes aware and learns to how to partake in his or her often chaotic social, emotional world. Your child will never be able to figure this out on his or her own-this is the nature of a delay, and the reason we work to provide therapy and care for our children. Your child is not learning isolated skills, but is learning to acculturate and become integrated into real life through your guidance.

The following are the parameters that constitute the *Senior and Junior partnership*:

- Building the Senior and Junior relationship requires at least two people. You will want to stick to just yourself (Mom or Dad) and your child to start, so both of you can get used to your new roles. If there is a two-parent/caregiver household, each parent/caregiver works separately at first as the child's Senior partner. When the parent is comfortable, and the child is comfortable working with each of you separately, then you can both join into the same partnership.

- One person needs to be an experienced partner- the adult who is fluent in the social arena, and the other, your child who is the junior partner who is not. Later, once the child is more socially proficient, siblings and peers can be taught how to come into the mix.
- There is a *relationship* that develops between the Senior and the Junior partner. Focus on the relationship and not on tasks.
- Both Senior and Junior partners partake in an active, reciprocal-back and forth *experience together*.
- Both roles are interdependent. As the Senior Partner, you can't do your role successfully if your Junior Partner is not doing his or her role and vice versa. Do not compensate for your child.
- The partnered relationship takes place in real time in socially-based authentic settings. Home is ideal, but the classroom or other environments are fine, as long as you make the interaction authentic.
- The Senior Partner needs to use a communication style which supports the sharing of experiences (more on the communication style you will need in ingredient #3).

- There is an inherent social goal for each engagement.
- There is a critical thinking goal inherent for each engagement.

In The Social Diet, the job of the Senior Partner is critical. You bring your experience and your knowledge to the table. As the leader, it is your job to make sure your child is engaged with you, and, eventually, with the world. The role of Senior Partner should *not* to be confused with facilitator or entertainer for the child. This is an important distinction. All too often I see adults used this way without even thinking about it or being aware of it. If you are allowing the child to use you to fulfill his or her needs, you are *not* acting as the Senior Partner. If you allow the child to do things alone (often adults sees this as promoting independence), you are not doing the job of Senior Partner. If you are doing all the work and allowing the child to be entertained, you are not in the Senior position. Your child might be very happy with you, but will not be learning from you.

For your *Senior and Junior Partnership* to be successful, the child needs to be what we call "regulated." A regulated child is one who is:

- Aware of the Senior Partner
- Able to focus (mentally and physically) on the Senior Partner
- Accepts to be led by the Senior Partner

- Contributes something positive to the *reciprocal interaction* or experience

Please Note:

Don't be alarmed if your child or student is not yet ready to do this. Most children who start The Diet are not regulated or ready. Don't worry if this is the case for you. Most kids are not ready to be guided initially. They want to have control and are used to getting it. However, as in all parenting relationships, this will need to change, if you want to engage in The Social Diet (or any healthy parenting relationship). The good news is that in most cases, this behavior can be turned around. This is where most children need to begin the journey. Do not worry if your family is also beginning at this point.

Remember, ***you cannot guide a child who is not ready to be guided***. In most cases, both you and the child will need to take on new roles and responsibilities, which can be challenging. At the same time, however, nothing is more rewarding than establishing a trusted Senior and Junior Partnership with your child.

Relationships Equal Happiness

Your children don't need more "stuff." They need *you*. They don't have to live in a big house, have the nicest toys, and the nicest clothes. While that is somewhat enjoyable, most of what we give our children is superficial. Tangible material gifts will not help form a mentally, socially-connected healthy child. In fact, it might even make it worse. I use the following as an example:

How many of us have our children begging at some point or another for something that they absolutely *need* and could not possibly live without or their lives will be over? At least, they feel as if it will. My daughter practically broke me down when she was in 8th grade, pleading, "All my other friends have phones. Mom, can you *please, please, please,* buy me a phone?" At the end of the school year, for her Bat-Mitzvah, my sister bought her one (to my chagrin).

Well, if you were to ask Yael (pronounced Ya-el) if her phone makes her happy, she wouldn't miss a beat and would shout out, "Yes!" However, from my perspective, it was not a good thing for two main reasons. First, after having the phone for a couple of months, I noticed that my daughter's behaviors started to change dramatically. Before she had the phone, Yael was basically a happy-go-lucky child. She was a girl who begged me for Friday night sleepovers with friends so she could (physically) be with her peers, a girl who loved going outside to explore, a girl who would quickly gravitate to her favorite physical pastimes. After her phone, she turned into almost a different person. Those things that she enjoyed most, practically disappeared. She became one of those girls who is perfectly "happy" to stay in her room all day and night on her phone. I began to become very worried. As if this symptom was not bad enough, I noticed that she became much more irritable and moody whenever she had spent too much time on her phone. It became clear to me that my daughter was not developmentally ready for the emotional fortitude required to navigate the forces of social media and everything that comes with it, as we know there is a great deal of drama that occurs as a byproduct of being "connected."

In the end, did the cell phone bring her happiness? No, it did not. Not only that, but it did her harm. It is important to realize that kids (and even lots of adults) are not able to know what they need to make themselves happier. They are not developmentally ready to know what they need. It is our job to make these decisions for them. This does not mean that phones, or social media sources, are a bad thing, but merely that my child was not developmentally ready at that time to use the tool she had wanted so badly. So, if your child begs you for a toy or tool, and throws a fit, while the *feeling* your child has is very real in his or her mind, it's just the need for the next fix. After the initial novelty fades, he or she will be in search of his next material pursuit.

Your child's basic human needs can only be fed by people, real people, in real life. There is no other replacement, and there is no other way. No amount of material goods, no amount of knowledge, and no amount of time they spend connected to a device can satiate their most basic needs. As long as we remain human, the only way to get our foundational needs met is through face-to-face contact with other social beings. This is increasingly difficult in modern society, for those who are NT and non-NT alike. Parents are the first ones with the honor of feeding these needs of their children. If the parents' needs are not being met and nurtured, they will not be able to fulfill their own child's needs. We cannot give something to someone else if we don't first have it ourselves.

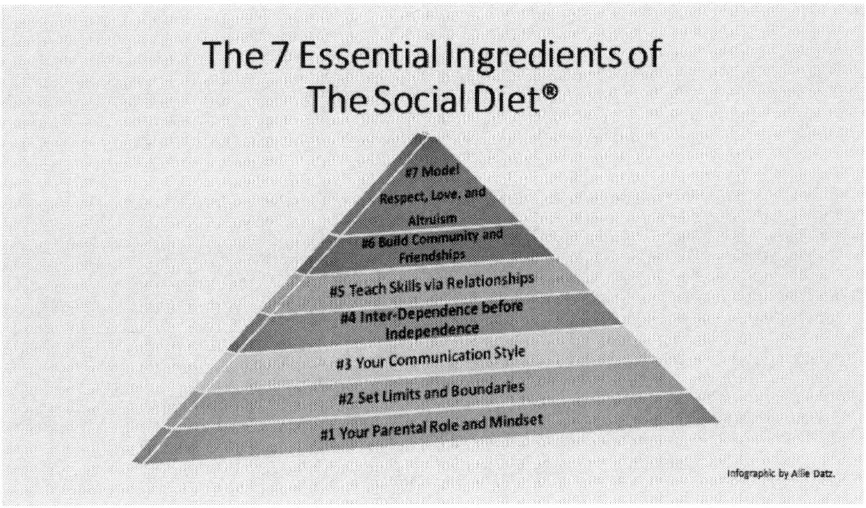

• CHAPTER 5 •

The Seven Key Ingredients of a Successful Social Diet

As with any kind of diet, you want to make sure that you are setting yourself up for success. There will be some good days and some not-so-good days-- that is life and that is *okay*. Like all diets, this one won't be followed perfectly, nor will you be capable of doing it perfectly on your first attempts. Keep going. You just want to make sure you have more good days than bad.

In order for your Social Diet® process to be successful, there are seven key ingredients which are essential. Each ingredient is critical if you want to make the most of your diet. As with any diet, if you cheat you will not get the results you are after. So, what happens if you are not strict about The Social Diet? You can make some improvements if you are missing an ingredient or two, but know that you and your child will not be benefiting from it in the same way as if you follow the diet the way it is designed. For this reason, consider that it takes all seven key ingredients for your recipe—The Social Diet—to work.

Ingredient Number 1: Your Parental Role and Mindset

Your Relationship is Key: The Gift of Connecting

I cannot think of a more precious gift in life than the gift of being and feeling connected to others. It doesn't matter where you are, what you are doing, or what you want to teach your child, you must first establish a strong emotional bond with your child. Your close relationship is the glue of your child's future social, emotional and cognitive development. The stronger your relationship, the further your child will be able to go in life.

Your Parental Role

Understanding Your Parental Role:

Being a parent IS the hardest job in the world. The responsibility and honor of forming another human is immense. Life prior to children is vastly different than life after. With this change comes, of course, uncertainty. Some of us do better than others with change. For some, parenthood might be a welcome anticipatory change, for others, it might be pretty scary, and for some, a combination of both or anywhere in between. This is especially true for those of us who might have special children with special needs. In this case, some will be able to handle these massive changes positively, but for others, the change can feel insurmountable to the point of sheer fear, paralysis, adrenal fatigue. In short, it's easy to be very overwhelmed!

Each one of us will feel what we feel, and all of these feelings are valid and necessary for us to work through and acknowledge *how* we feel, and *why* we feel as we do. It's critical to remember, though, that you have a choice about how to *react* to this change. The impact of the changes from parenting a non-neurotypical child will completely depend on you. Since you probably don't live in a vacuum, this change will also greatly impact all the people in your life—your family, friends, colleagues, and acquaintances. Before *doing* anything, before simply reacting to what is happening and going into your automatic mode, **Stop, Think and be Thoughtful**.

This new role of parenthood is huge. It deserves and needs the time for you to think about what this means for you, your partner, your family and everyone else. Most of us are so busy reacting and putting out the fires (because there will always be these fires to put out), that we fail to pause, take a breath and think first about what we need to do in terms of the big picture. We need to remember that "How I show up today, matters for what will show up tomorrow and in the future." We prepare so much for other things: a wedding, a trip, a presentation we need to give, our job or career. Yet when it comes to how we handle how we parent, we often don't give ourselves that same importance of preparing.

However, raising a child demands preparation. One day, you don't have a child, then the next day you deliver your first baby and then, suddenly, you are a parent. This is no small change. You owe it to yourself and your family to take the time to prepare for this, and to really take this in.

Parenting isn't simply *doing,* it's a lot of preparation behind the scenes. Your role needs to be deliberate and thoughtful.

I recommend that you spend some time really thinking about it on your own and/or with your spouse or partner. Think about the following:

- Being a parent will always mean a change in your live(s).
- What will this change mean to you personally?
- What will this change mean to your spouse and other family members?
- Realize that with change you will need to adopt new roles, new ways of thinking and doing things. Is what you've done in the past still working? If not, why not? Do you need a new technique?
- How can I remain empowered and flexible?
- What do I need to do to take care of myself?
- What do I need to take care of my partner?
- What do I need to take care of my child and/or my other children?

Most of us spend the first 18 years of our lives in school or in an academic setting, and then if we go to college, we spend at least four more years accumulating more "knowledge." We spend years developing our minds to accumulate and retain knowledge, discovering what we think we will need to be successful in life, yet many of us have never taken one course in parenting. We don't spend time learning how to take care of what we most treasure in life: our families and our children.

Isn't this strange when you really think about it? Can you imagine the difference it might make if we took the same amount of time to become a lawyer, dentist, office manager, or CEO of a company, and put the same amount of time and energy into raising our children? What would this look like? How could this impact our role of parenthood?

It's really mind-boggling when I think about it. Most of us just kind of "wing it" and fall back on how we were raised by our own parents. Well, that is fine and well if we had exceptional parents to model after.... but what if we didn't? What if our situation, or our children's neurological profile, is different than our experiences growing up? I would bet that most of us were not raised by "Exceptional parents," but rather, by parents that "just did the best that they could." Adding in attempting to negotiate difficult delays in emotion and behavior, and it's very easy to see why parents of non-neurotypical children get so frustrated. If we apply this to other settings, the strangeness of the request becomes clear.

What if your boss at a new job hired you without looking at your resume or experience, and then approached you on your first day and said, "Well, just wing it." You would have no background, no specified education or certification, no experience, but could only do the best you can. Crazy, right? Completely not possible and overwhelming. Why do we accept this scenario when it comes to having and parenting children, especially non-NT children?

The role that we take on for our children is paramount to the people they will become later in life. First and foremost, we are our children's guides to the outside world. We have the honor and responsibility to help form our children's values and emotional well-being.

As with all parenting, before jumping into any therapy, approach, or method, you must do your homework. Often, we don't like even the idea of homework, but we must become those savvy consumers who do their research from reliable sources, and who figure out what we want based on our own beliefs and values, not what others tell you that you should be doing. While other's opinions might count and be well intentioned, only you know what is best for your child. If you don't, that is just a sign that you need more research and education in your child's difficulties, so that you can make informed intelligent decisions. Don't just follow the masses. You must do your homework and decide what is important for you and your child right now, and equally important, how the decisions you make now will impact your child's future.

I am a big picture person. When it comes to decisions for my kids, I ask myself a simple question which helps me decide what to do. I say, "*Will this choice make my child a better person when he is older, will this choice matter when he or she is an adult.?*" For me, a person's character is the most important value for their future. *"Will this choice matter later in life?"* also helps me make even complex questions easier. In the modern world, there are so many unnecessary distractions, and we are so overwhelmed by information and sensory overload, that it is no wonder it is difficult to know where to spend our energy and time, and what information and techniques to focus upon. In my opinion, there is so much "noise" out there that is in our face and ears everyday, it has made us *numb*. I fear we as a society and as individuals, are less likely to see clearly and make the more important decisions such as my child is suffering "What should I do?", and find it easier and more enticing to choose a superficial quick fix to the problem, only to find that indeed it doesn't work long term and was just another distraction or a ban- aid solution to a much deeper problem.

We, as parents, need to stop running around and living in the rat race, and we must stop the reacting game. We need thoughtful, reflective, solutions-- which will probably be more difficult and more time consuming, as educating ourselves always takes more time than to go with what others tell you, but which solutions will have a long term, life improving impact. Usually this means more work for the parent, but, *parenting is work*: it is the hardest work one will ever have in their life. It is an investment, but it's an investment worth the time and effort it takes to help our children progress.

You are the Role Model:

The Power of Positive and Negative Behaviors

An important factor, which often goes unnoticed, is that our choices reflect our values and beliefs, even though we may not be consciously aware that they do so. These values and beliefs get passed down to our kids, again perhaps unconsciously on our part, and on the part of our children. Everything which we do and say, our children are studying and modeling, even our neurodiverse children whom we might not think are paying attention. Believe me, they *are* paying attention. They might not be following your words, but they are modeling your behaviors, your body language, and your actions and *re*actions to your world. So, your choices not only reflect you, but also your children's most probable outcomes and choices in the future.

These typically unseen nuances in behavior are teaching your kids how you model your ability to cope with stressful situations. Don't get bogged down by expecting yourself to be perfect because of these worries, however. Every decision and every act or action a parent takes impacts their child on some level (either positively, negatively or neutrally), and you cannot control every action or reaction, both from yourself or your community. This is not a book about child psychology nor am I an expert in this area. My expertise lies in knowing that everything we do, everything we see, say, don't say, hear and touch is information we humans take in and what we use to create meaning. It is important to recognize this in our parental role. The choices we make, or don't make have direct impact on our kids.

To begin The Social Diet, we need to create the space for, and the intention of, starting something new. Getting yourself ready for success starts long before day one of the Diet. You need to get geared up in your way of thinking and behaving before taking any action. A large portion of this is realizing that the purpose of The Social Diet is for you, the parent, to create an immersion approach to real life for your child. Your top priority is to create a life for your child which immerses them in rich social experiences which will teach him or her how to relate with others in the world. This is our number one goal in all parenting relationships, and more so with a special needs child. Most likely, this means that you will have to make changes to your family's life. You already have made many changes, but these will make your progress more tangible. It is probable that you will need to recalibrate what you are doing, how you are doing it and be willing to change things up in order to prioritize and support your child's needs—but this is what you do for your non-NT child anyway. Parents of non-NT kids learn early about adaptations and changing their expectations, but we want to be able to reset and make sure that your path is headed in the direction you prefer. This means educating ourselves as parents in our current thought patterns, analyzing our state of mind, and looking at our actions to see how they may or may not be serving us or our family.

The starting point for doing The Social Diet hinges upon your ability to reflect.

This piece is critical and we need to give ourselves this time for reflection. Most of us are still functioning on a subconscious level about the way we communicate, what causes our actions, and how this impacts our children's learning. In order to be able to carry out The Social Diet you must become conscious of these motivations, because it requires you to learn a completely new way of interacting and communicating with your child. This is easier than it seems, but takes conscious effort.

Most of us think that if only the *child* would change, things would be a whole lot better. This is, of course, the wrong mindset. Ironically, your child is not the problem. In order for The Social Diet to even get off the ground, your mindset must be that it is not the child who has to change. Your child will only change if you, the parent, change first. You will soon realize that your child will improve tremendously when you are willing to reflect and adapt to a new set of communication tools.

Take on the Commitment

Having the right mindset for The Social Diet requires the proper dedication and commitment. Like most diets there are no quick fixes. If there were easy solutions to teaching and learning the social piece for our children, we would have found it already. The truth of the matter is that this piece is *difficult* but *not impossible*. It takes a long time, and like any diet it requires fortitude and commitment to be successful. We live in a society which wants quick fixes, and magic wand answers. This doesn't work for any family, especially not our own. So besides being willing to take a good hard look at your own behaviors and communication style, you will need to embrace the fact that this is a long-term commitment. The good news is that once you become proficient at The Social Diet it becomes instinctual. You may need to tweak some strategies to apply to your family needs, but once you have mastered all the ingredients, you are well on your way.

Take an Active Role

Another important component of having the right mindset for The Social Diet is to realize that you, the parent, play a very critical and active role in your child's social growth. The Social Diet will teach you how to build a new kind of relationship with your child. This requires lots of hands-on work. Your job is to be your child's teacher, and as such you will need to play and be active. You are not teaching your child just a social skill, but teaching them how to be truly socially engaged. This requires interaction on both your and your child's part. I will teach you how to make this possible.

Set Aside Ample Time

In order to have the right mindset to begin The Social Diet, you must be willing to set aside enough time during your day to practice these new techniques. What is the proper amount of time? It varies from family to family, depending on the parents' and child's learning curve. Certainly, you don't want to be doing The Social

Diet with your child 24/7. That is not very realistic, and you would both burn out very quickly. However, as with any diet, the more time you spend working on it, the better the results for the most part. I suggest starting out slowly, but steadily. At first you just want to get your feet wet. Once you feel comfortable you will want to do more. As you want to set yourself up for success, choose an amount of time that is doable initially.

I recommend you only do 10 minutes per day for five days during your first two weeks. On week three, build up to 20 minutes a day for five days. Try that on for size and see how you do. About week six, go for 30 minutes per day for five days. Once you feel comfortable with that, you can build up to an hour or more per day, five times a week. You are building your muscles here. Once it becomes part of your routine, you will be doing it without even realizing it.

The key is to adapt The Social Diet into your lifestyle. At first it may feel a bit awkward. Changing your own behavior and communication may not seem natural initially. But, give it time. After around six months of The Social Diet, you will be seasoned enough that you will start incorporating it into your family's daily life. It won't feel new or confusing anymore and living it will get easier.

Set High Expectations

I know that every good parent wants the best for their child. Part of having the right mindset is setting your expectations high. Our expectations play a huge part in our children's growth. Research confirms that children perform to adult expectations. If you give excuses why you think your child cannot do something, he or she will meet your lowered expectation. Conversely, if you expect your child to do well and demand the work to do so, chances are good that your child will be able to meet your expectations. How we think is the primary factor in what kinds of outcomes we will have. So, while you want your child's goals to be achievable and realistic, set your mind on success.

Set Your Priorities – Create a Social Immersion Approach

Let's revisit an important question to ask yourself: "Is what my child is doing or learning today really going to help him in a *socially* meaningful way when he/she is an adult?" The social piece must remain the top priority for your child. In today's world it is very easy to be pulled in several directions at the same time. Remember you need to stop *doing*. Carting your child from therapy to therapy or from one activity to another might not yield a social child. Spending time *being* together in a deliberate way will. Make that your priority!

I set my priorities with my son, Ylann, when he was 2 years old , at his initial diagnosis. The most important thing to me was that my son would become an active member of society-- that he would learn "how to be" and act in the world. As such, I made sure that how he spent each day would be my priority. If I wanted my son to know how to be in the world, my job as his parent was to make sure that his daily living experience prioritized these goals. Because of my training, I knew that the only way Ylann was going to become fluent in society was to give him a heavy dose of real-life social engagements. This meant having him interact as much as possible with other people. So, I took him everywhere with me.

You, as the parent of a non-NT child, immediately understand why this was fraught with complications! Many of us bear the strain of social interactions from before our child received their diagnosis, and the added glares and narrowed eyes from strangers in public from their assumption at our ineffective or permissive parenting. Each of us has, to a different degree, been worried about public tantrums or behavior unacceptable in our culture or society. However, even at the risk of his having meltdowns, I exposed Ylann to many different places and experiences. I'll be honest-- it would have been easier to leave him at home with my husband, but I knew deep down that Ylann needed practice being out in the real world. I, too, needed the practice, so that one day we could be a successful team. I had the mindset that it didn't matter what other people thought; I was going to teach my child how to be in the world. I set my expectations high, and I didn't let my child's behavior dictate what I was or was not going to do. This was not easy.

I remember telling Ylann's preschool teachers, "I am not going to be impressed if Ylann knows the alphabet or any other academic skill. What will impress me is that he becomes an active participant in his class." They looked at me and I explained, "I don't want my son to be the one later in life who everyone comes to only when they have a technology problem. I want them to want to be with Ylann, and become his true friend." I knew, even then, that if I wanted my son to have friends, I needed to make that our focus.

Become the Professional

As well-meaning as the professionals are, they do not know your child as well as you do if you are doing your job to be connected to your child. The more you educate yourself the better off your child will be. Do your homework and become an integral part of your child's journey. Remember that people will come and go during your child's lifetime, but you are not going anywhere. Stay informed, stay active, and invest in yourself.

I can remember when we first got Ylann's diagnosis, I was hoping that the professionals were going to take over and tell me what I needed to do. It is a terribly helpless feeling to be going through a sudden grief, and something you do not yet know anything about. To some degree they did- the professionals stepped in and told me what, in their experience, needed to be done. Probably the same is true in your experience. We have to realize, however, that autism is a relatively new field and professionals do not have all the answers. If something is important to you, or something doesn't seem right to you, you must let your voice be heard. It's okay to question the professionals you encounter, even your own professional knowledge and opinions. As with any kind of education, autism requires that you put the time in to learn as much as you can, so you are in a position of strength. My mother still tells me, "Stacy, the squeaky wheel gets the oil." She is right, and informed parents know best! It is your job to get involved and be in a position of strength, so you can effectively advocate for your child.

What Kind of Mindset Do You Have?
Undergo a Paradigm Shift

Another critical component to having the right mindset for The Social Diet requires that you welcome a paradigm shift which moves away from skill-based instruction and forges ahead with a socially-based interactive immersion approach. This does not mean that you are not teaching skills, but they are the hidden skills needed for your child to become a participating social partner in a world which is social. We need to do this by preparing ourselves to be our child's leader. After that we do this by creating an active and engaged environment for our child. Forming a true learning partnership with your child is key.

The 4 Mindsets:

I am a firm believer that we can we can do anything we put our minds to. Through years of working with families, I have come up with four different mindsets which parents have after receiving a diagnosis. They are 1) *The Denial Mindset, 2) The Victim* and/or *The Blaming Mindset, 3) The Angry and/or Fearful Mindset,* and 4) *The Empowered Mindset.*

Imagine if your mindset could talk to you…. because it actually does. You dialogue with your subconscious mind hundreds of times each day, but you probably are unaware of it. You could say that your mindset is that little voice inside of you which drives how you think, feel, and approach your life. Your mindset is so strong that if you really start to pay attention to it, it can predict what happens to you in the present, and what will happen to you in your future.

It has forever been true that how we think and feel determine how we live our life. If you think you can't do something, you probably will not succeed. Conversely if you feel confident about something chances are that you will be successful in that area. The same holds true for how you feel and think about your child. There is a direct link from your type of mindset to your own child's way of thinking, acting and behavior. For example, you just got the news that your child is *a*typical. What is your reaction? What kind of mindset do you have? Look at the first section of phrases below and find what kind of mindset you typical have.

The Denial Mindset-

- "There is nothing wrong. I don't care what they say."
- "If we just wait it out, she'll grow out of it."
- "His teacher doesn't know what she's talking about."
- "I was like that as a kid, and I turned out *just fine*!"

The Victim and/or Blaming Mindset

- "I knew this was going to happen. Everything always happens to me."
- "Why did this happen? Why us? Why does this have to happen to our son?"
- "It's my husband's fault. His father was crazy."
- "We never had anything like this in *my* family!"
- "This is horrible. Nothing ever will be the same again."

The Angry and/or Fearful Mindset-

- "What are we going to do? I can't handle this."
- "We will never be able to pay for all of this therapy."
- "We don't have money for this."
- "What about our child's future?"
- "What is going to happen to her?"
- "Will he ever be 'normal'? What if he's not, then what?"

I recognize that humans go through natural emotions when they are faced with stressful and painful news. The grief cycle is a healthy process, when you do not get stuck in one point or another within it. Denial, victimhood, and pointing the finger do serve a purpose, but only *initially.* We are not meant to stay in this shocked phase, where we are incapacitated to deal with the new reality of bad news. Shock, sorrow, bargaining, and anger are very natural human states of grieving. But, if you get stuck in any of these places for too long, the outcome will be staying stuck. This will always be the most painful place to reside. In the long run, nothing positive can come out of these mindsets.

If you fall under this category of mindset, do the physical and emotional work that you have to do in order to get past it. Simply hoping that things will get better, without any action, does not help. In some cases, seeking professional help can be useful, but only if you have a positive attitude about this potential help. If you don't think anyone can help you, they also won't be able to. If a person wants to stay stuck or will not do the work to progress through the grief cycle, they will stay stuck. This is the path of least resistance, one where we don't have to deal with the sadness, and where we get a "free pass" from responsibility. In my opinion, wanting to be a responsible parent would propel that person to move past this inertia state. Unfortunately, I've witnessed many who choose to stay here to everyone's detriment.

The Denial, Victim/Blaming, Angry/Fearful mindsets are all negative ones. Make no mistake about it, your children will pick up on how you cope with stress. Whether we like it or not, our behavior is what our children see, and will model, in their day to day interactions. I see this repeatedly in clients. When something doesn't go the child's way, they are quick to put the blame on anyone and everyone but themselves. "It's Bobby's fault; I didn't touch it." "Mom, this isn't fair; My teacher gave me an "F." "It's not my fault! I didn't know..."

I don't think we can be effective parents, and not see this when it manifests in our children. Our children are, for good and ill, mirrors of ourselves. If you don't like the behavior you see, instead of blaming them and being harsh with them, first check in with your own state of mind.

Think of it this way: Many of us can tell immediately the emotional state of the person we are engaged with. Everyone who has a significant other knows what I am talking about. You can tell if your partner is happy, upset, indifferent, or excited. Well, so can your kids, including those with social emotional issues. Don't make the mistake of assuming that because your child is non-NT, he isn't picking up on what you are doing, how you are doing it, and the energy that you are giving off. If you are calm and collected, your child will know. If you are in a reactive, scared, or uncertain state, they will feel that, and take that in. If this is the "normal" way of your behavior, chances are your child will pick this up and recreate their "normal" to be much like yours. The worst mindset of all, however, is the "I can't, you can't, he can't, we can't, they can't."

The Can't or Will not Mindset

- "I can't do that."
- "He can't do that."
- "They won't have friends."
- "That's too hard for him."

- "I could never do that."
- "That's impossible. That will never happen."
- "Are you kidding me? Yeah, right."
- "Who are you kidding?"
- "Don't expect too much."
- "That most likely will not become a reality."
- "Why are you even thinking like that?"
- "You're setting yourself up for failure."

Sadly, this list can go on indefinitely, and is ready-made for us to think this is our reality. No doubt this a defense mechanism we have developed, often after hearing those same words from professionals caring for our child. We believe that if we don't expect it, we won't be disappointed when we don't get it. If we can't possibly achieve it, why even bother doing it? To act any other way wouldn't be reasonable and could even be construed as cruel. After all, when it comes to parenting, how can we ask our children to accomplish anything they simply can't do? Who would ever do such a thing? (Or so the thinking goes.)

What we fail to understand is that this way of "un-achieving" or lowering our expectation brings the bar to a lower standard which quickly becomes our norm, which then becomes what we truly believe is our reality. Not because we *shouldn't* expect more, but we are taught to think that anything else is impossible, and, as such, it almost becomes impossible to think any other way.

This *Can't or Will Not* mentality can have devastating consequences to your child's quality of life, not to mention your own. If we don't think our kids with autism can have friends, parents do not foster a child's environment to entertain this idea. Why invite any friends over when your child can't relate? Why push for playdates when your child is unable to play with other kids? Why should a parent expect their child to be able to participate at the dinner table because "he needs to get up and move around?" Why expect your child to learn how to behave because she has sensory issues? Kids, however, will always perform up to our adult expectations. If we set the bar low, they will reach it. If we set it high, they will reach that too. I will never forget when the Assistant Director of a huge school district in another state told me quite matter-of-factly, "Well, you know, kids on the spectrum can't generalize."

"What?" I said, taken aback.

"Kids on the spectrum cannot generalize."

I was shocked at her bluntness, but more disturbing was that this was her belief as someone who held high status in a very highly populated special-needs community. If she really believed this, and she is a leader, what would her cohorts think? How does this attitude trickle down to the parents? If those who are the gate-keepers and in a position of authority believe in a certain way which undermines our children, we are treading in very dangerous waters. How does it serve our leaders all the way down to our neighbors to believe uniformly in the low capabilities of our children?

What is wrong with raising the bar? What is wrong with having a drive to be ambitious, and what is wrong with pushing our own personal limits? For non-neurotypical children, as well as neurotypical children, if a parent is going to arbitrarily set the bar low because they think their children are "disadvantaged," they will never know their true potential.

We are inadvertently training our kids to be followers rather than to be leaders. I want more for you, and for your families. I think that parents who do not challenge their children do a them a disservice, because that bar may not be at the level of aspiration that the child could otherwise easily obtain. Why not encourage the child to move the bar, to have to put some effort in? When we take over their lives without inspiring them, we limit and stifle their future, and this is an all-to-common tendency for parents of special needs children.

We condition them to be "less than." We make it okay that normal is average, when in reality there is no normal. Average is the sum of all the successes, divided by the number of candidates. That attitude is grossly unfair, demoralizing, and debilitating. It is not inspirational. It is not forward thinking.

The Behind-the-Scenes Essentials to Having an Empowered Mindset

While any one of us may experience these negative mindsets, you must know that *none* of them will ever result in healthy emotional or behavioral outcomes. When it comes to dealing with difficult behavioral, social, or emotional issues with your child, no amount of denial, blame, playing victim to fear will take away the pain you are feeling, nor will it yield the very thing that you need—solutions. The longer you remain in the above three mindsets, the longer you and your child will be suffering.

So why do so many of us hold onto blaming others, being the victim, hold on to denial or fear so tightly? Why do we behave like this? The answer is simple and human: in the short term it's easier and less painful, or so we think. If we are not in the business of blaming others, denying difficult situations, or fearful and angry, that means that we will have to *Take Responsibility*.

I believe that the number one bane in our American culture is that we don't want to take responsibility. If something is wrong, we look to make it the other person's fault. There are many grownups who look like they have their act together…when things are going well. As soon as something goes wrong, however, they are in reactive, blame-the-other-guy mode. If something happens to your child, it's human nature to blame something or someone. However, the irony is that taking an action of responsibility will promote better health for yourself and everyone around you. It will alleviate pain in the long term, instead of it festering inside your body and mind in perpetuity. I am amazed at the energy money, and time people spend avoiding their pain, self-medicating with drinking, smoking, drugs, over eating, and other behaviors which do not address their sorrow directly. As a society, we will go to the depths of depression, anxiety, or even killing ourselves in order to not have to face our pain and take responsibility for it. Human nature is very complex. It wants to take the easier way out, thinking that will help us, but in the long run this damages us even further, and prolongs the pain and the inevitable sorrow. We can't run from ourselves or our children no matter how hard we try. It takes a mature, courageous, responsible human being not to point the finger, not to need to know why, not to play the victim or feel paralyzed in front of difficult life circumstances. It takes an enormous amount of energy, time and effort, persistence, and the ability to accept previous failures, and to be able to come out on the other side to *responsibility*.

The only way to become a responsible adult parent is to let go of everything else, and face the pain and fear, both for yourself and that you hold for your child. This can be an arduous journey, but you *can* achieve it. The first step is to become more aware and curious, without judgment. Most of us cannot be fully objective with our own behaviors. We can see others' actions and reactions much more easily than our own. Why do you think therapists have their own therapist? Why did I use a parenting coach when I was raising my children? Everyone needs help- because we can't see what we don't see. We can't change or improve upon anything that we don't know about or understand. It often takes trusted others' perspectives, to point out how they see us. The same is true for how we parent. Often, we don't notice that we are not showing up for our children in a positive way. Most of us know that we parent the same way our parents did, even if we didn't like what they did. We can't help ourselves; it's in our DNA. That is what we lived with; that is who we are.

To become different than who we have already been conditioned to be takes monumental work. The kind of mindset you choose (and yes, it is a choice) to embrace will affect everything that happens between you and your child. If you get nothing else out of this book, I want you to understand this point: you get to choose how you interact with your child, and what mindset you have in parenting.

I completely believe the following proverb by Frank Outlaw to be true:

"Watch your words, they become your thoughts,
Watch your thoughts, they become your actions,
Watch your actions, they become your habits,
Watch your habits, they become your character,
Watch your character, it becomes your destiny!"

And, may I add, the destiny of your children.

This point is essential, to me, if you are ever going to turn things around and be the responsible, connected, thoughtful parent that you want to be for your child. The trick is, most of us, maybe all of us, need help with this. *It is not a sign of weakness to seek professional help*. It is a sign of love and courage for yourself, your partner, and your family. Admitting you are stuck in an unproductive mindset and that you need help is extremely brave and honorable. Sometimes this takes parenting books, sometimes therapy, and sometimes medications, in order to help you on your path. The brain is, after all, a portion of the body, and must be treated as such.

The Empowered and Responsible Mindset

Imagine the difference in you, your partner, your family, and especially your children if you had an empowered mindset. In this mindset you not only take responsibility, but you are open to learning and experiencing new things. In and empowered and responsible mindset you realize that no matter what you are facing, there is chance for growth. There may even be silver linings and blessings if you look deep enough. In this mindset you might hear yourself saying phrases such as:

- "Whatever it takes, I can handle it."
- "I get to be an amazing role model for my kid."
- "I get to educate myself and learn something new and important for our family."

- "I get to be a leader and learn and grow as a person."
- "I am going to have the opportunity to learn persistence, courage, tenacity, vulnerability, and empowerment."
- "Even though this might be hard at first, I am determined to do whatever it takes to be the parent I need to be."
- "If I don't know something I will find out and ask for help."
- "I see an opportunity to be closer to my family."

Life, no matter what, is stressful. If we are living a full life, we cannot avoid it. Having a child who faces challenges is, of course, stressful but you have to keep telling yourself *you can* handle these difficulties. It's important to pay attention to the internal dialogue which accompanies stress. You must be aware of what you are telling yourself, and other people. It's okay to be upset, and incredibly frustrated even, but you will need practice choosing an empowered, responsible mindset instead of reverting back to negative thinking, which is so much easier to do. This sort of empowered mindset, especially after sudden grief, does not come automatically to most people. There are very few Pollyanna's out there who choose to have a positive outlook when life throws them curve balls-- and having a non-NT kid is a *big* curve ball in life. We must, instead, deliberately practice thinking more positively and coming up with solutions which will empower us, if we are ever going to break the pattern of negative thinking. Negative thinking, and thinking about worst-case scenarios, will completely take over if we let it. Anxiety is natural in parents who have to be constantly vigilant in order to protect a child who might have no concept of danger, or fear, or remembrance of past complications. However, while we protect our children, we have to combat the urge towards panic and constant anxiety, and not give into it. If you practice the empowered and responsible mindset enough, you will be able to change the way you think and see opportunities no matter what life circumstances you face.

How do you handle stress in your life at home, in the workplace, and in public with your kids? The following questions are there to help you become more aware of your own behavior and how you handle it stress. The first step to any kind of behavioral change is to *become aware* of what you do. So, please, be as open and honest with yourself as possible.

Questions to Think About:

- How do you handle stress in general?
- How do you handle stress with your child(ren)?
- How do you handle stress with your partner (if applicable)?
- How do you handle stress at work?
- How often do you get stressed or overwhelmed on an average day?
- What situations make you feel overwhelmed?
- How long do these stressful periods last?

- Do you feel like you have a healthy way to deal with your stress?

When faced with stress, think about the following:

- How do you behave?
- Are you reactive or are you able to remain composed despite the stress?
- How do you express yourself? What kinds of words do you use?
- What tone of voice do you use? What kind of body language are you displaying?
- What does your face look like?
- Are you aware of any emotions you are exhibiting?
- If so, what kind of emotions come up for you?
- Do you feel completely overwhelmed or do you feel that you can handle it?
- What is your demeanor? Would you feel comfortable if a stranger acted this way?
- Is your way of handling stress demonstrative of how you would like your kids to learn how to handle it? (This is the most important question of all.)

I suggest that you really take the time to answer these questions. You may not like what you notice or what comes up for you. ***That is okay***. Taking an honest look at your behavior is not easy; in fact, it can be painful. Once you reflect on these questions, I suggest that you ask a trusted person in your life who knows you intimately to answer these questions according to what they see. Chances are, you will be surprised at what you hear. Often, we tend to see ourselves differently than others see us. (Just ask a friend, or a colleague to describe you, and you will see what I mean.) What's important here is that you become more reflective and thoughtful about your own reactions and behaviors because this is what your children are seeing and learning.

Ask yourself before you address your child, "Am I grounded and peaceful, or am I reacting?" "Am I modeling thoughtful behavior, or am I out of control?" This is the time to stop pointing fingers at whatever is bothering you, and do some self-examination. It takes a mature person to step back and take the time to observe his/her own behavior. Ask yourself, "What kind of behavior am I modeling for my child? "What kind of language am I using?" Is it soft and calm, or it is angry?

Ingredient Number 2: Setting Boundaries and Limits

No real learning or relationship can happen if your child is not ready to learn from you. Getting your child ready to accept your guidance is essential. It is by far the most crucial portion of The Social Diet. Turning your child around to be ready for guidance starts at home, with your ability to set limits and boundaries. Autism or other developmental delays may be a reason for poor behaviors--but we cannot let it be an *excuse.* Expect that your child will behave well and accept nothing less. I realize this can be the most challenging piece for families (and professionals too). Practically every family with which I have ever worked came to me wanting to find solutions for their child's inappropriate behaviors. I wish I could say that there is a magic bullet for this, but there is not. The behavioral piece is like a moving target. Just when you think you have figured it out, something new arises- but this is true with parenting any child, NT or non-NT. Appropriate behaviors are still something which I have to work on with my son every day.

Every family and every child is different, but there are certain guidelines which I can offer. If your child's behavior is so extreme that he is aggressive and has harmed himself or others, you need to seek in person, professional help. Our first priorities are the safety of your child and yourself as your child ages and therapy can help a great deal with those complications. If your child's behaviors are manageable, however, the following guidelines should be able to help.

Establish Household Rules

To change any behavior, we have to become aware of it. My first suggestion is that parents take a week observing what goes on at home. Take note of your child's behaviors, both good and bad. After a week of just noticing what goes on with you and your child, ask yourself what changes you would like to see happen.

With these things in mind, sit together with your partner or other caregiver, and discuss. Now, you are ready to establish the new and improved "Household Rules." Write down on a sheet of paper all the appropriate behaviors which you would like to see at home. On another sheet of paper, make a list of all the inappropriate behaviors which will no longer be tolerated. Discuss with your partner how you will handle your child's violations of inappropriate behavior, and how you will reinforce the behaviors you want. Note: I do not recommend a token reward system in most cases. Rewards should include fun things that you and your child can do together, instead of material objects or food.

When you and your partner are ready, call a "family meeting" where you can present your child(ren) with the new household rules and expectations. This doesn't need to be all doom and gloom-- the experience can be very positive! For children who are able to participate, I recommend making the lists of appropriate and inappropriate behaviors *together* as a project. You can get markers and poster board, so that everyone can participate, and then hang them up where all of you can see them. Tell your child(ren) that you are excited to start this process, because by enforcing this everyone will be able to get along so much better. Keep it upbeat and fun.

You may ask yourself, "But, how do I remain calm if my child is still out of control?" This worry is actually much more common than we think. There are many parents out who have a soft touch, and are calm and quiet and thoughtful-- all the good stuff we want. However, they may not always be like this. They might appear with a gentle persona in public and think that if they model this way of being, their child should see this and be able to mirror this. These parents are wonderful to have, but there is a drawback. Often they are *too* calm, too laid back, too accepting, or too understanding. These are the parents who often don't want confrontation, either because they themselves don't like it, or have been conditioned in their own families to avoid angering their own parent or caregivers. These parents are often extremely perceptive and know exactly what buttons or triggers will push their child over the edge to deregulation, and they avoid those things at all costs. Their subconscious thinking is, "We don't want to rock the boat, because poor Johnathan won't like it, and not only that, we will pay for it. This will create a scene, and/or a complete meltdown and we *don't* want that."

Often, the instinct of, "we don't want that" comes because we really don't know how to handle that sort of deregulation. Or, worse, we believe that we are doing our child a favor because we are keeping him calm. Instead, I want to teach you how to create an environment in which your child can become calm. There is no way to avoid all possible ways that a child could become surprised, scared, or otherwise overwhelmed as adults in society. Avoiding possible deregulation triggers is not the end goal for parenting. Instead, we want to teach children how to calm themselves, and how to ask for the help that they need and will need as adults.

"Stop Everything" Tips for the Over-Controlling Child:

A strategy which I use in the home environment with my clients is called the "Stop Everything Tips" for the over-controlling child. I got these tips during my RDI® training from Dr. Gutstein, and they have proven to be invaluable in my own home, and in that of my clients. Very often children with autism, ADD/ADHD, and like disorders can become hyperactive or disorganized in their actions. I am sure each of you has many examples of this. As our children's teachers, we do not want them to continue in this dysregulated state. Our job is to help them to recalibrate to a more organized way of thinking and behaving. We do this by co-regulating or partnering up with them in specific ways. When a child loses his focus, or moves himself away from the joint engagement, that is your cue to use the "Stop Everything Tips" below as a way to halt your child's over-zealous and dysregulated state.

Below is what you need to know and do:

1. Remember, compliance or being regulated is a prerequisite to teaching your child how to become a successful partner. They must be able to listen and follow through with you, first, in order to appropriately and happily engage with the outside world.
2. Do not let the word "Partner" throw you off. You are *not* equals. You are the adult. You are not your child's friend. You are the leader and teacher.
3. Do not allow your child to control you. If you feel like you do, the following steps are for you.

4. Do NOT make excuses for your child's poor behavior, "Oh, he's hungry, he's tired, he's still young. He'll grow out of it." Think to yourself, "Would I allow this behavior of a 16-year-old, neurotypical child?" Because that is what you need to prepare for *now*. The longer you wait before insisting your child behaves appropriately, the longer this ingredient will take to master. The younger your child, the easier it is. Do not put this ingredient off. Remember, you will not be able to continue with The Social Diet without it.
5. I can't emphasize this enough! Do not WAIT to begin this process!
6. Some (or a lot of) initial negativity is critical and expected in the early stages for some of the most controlling children. Just expect it, and welcome it as a sign that you are moving in the right direction. You must realize that change will be resisted until your child learns that you mean what you say and do, and you are consistent. Again, this resistance will be easier the younger your child is and the more consistent you are with setting limits and boundaries. If your child is over 10 years old, this step could take some time. Brace yourself for the power struggle. Your child has been able to get away with certain things before, for at least 10 years. Changing up the familiar family dynamics will not occur without a fight. This is okay, just expect it and be ready to hold your ground. If you are not *firm and consistent*, your child will know and take advantage. If this happens, spend the time to regroup and make the necessary changes which you can stick to.

Children at any age and with any cognitive ability can tell if you mean business or not. If you can't manage this part on your own, consult with a professional. It's that important to learn this new behavior, both for yourself and for your child.

7. Your child needs to begin to trust (not in terms of physical safety) that you are the Senior Partner and you can lead him to better way of showing up in the world. No child likes a dysregulated state (nor do adults for that matter). Your job is to accept that your child will be unhappy at first but there is no better gift you can give him or her than the ability to recover from disappointment. Our children need so much control in order to feel okay. We want to be able to teach them how to let go of their need to control, and be okay with the outcome. They will have to be able to deal with innumerable disappointments in life. We all need to be able to be okay that things are not perfect and they don't have to be. This is a reality you want your child to experience and overcome in positive ways.
8. You must guide your child away from the unhealthy need for control. Instead of entering a power struggle or worse, giving in to them, **Stop Everything!**

"Stop Everything" means: nothing else goes on until the child follows the adult's lead (meaning he is able to co-regulate with you) and is calm. To stop everything you will need to:

- Make sure your space is clear, so that the child cannot reach any object or people other than yourself.

- Sit or stand together until you (the adult) become the central focus of attention. This may require putting a young child on your lap. For older children you can sit next to them holding their hand or not—whichever is necessary for the child to stop everything. For teenagers you will need to work out an individual plan , which typically involves giving the child two choices, which you create for him. If he chooses not to participate, then consequences are set.

- Do not let your child get up or fidget. Stop Everything means that the child, and you, stop everything until the child is able to be completely calm. Sit with him as long as it takes for him to stop resisting, and quiet his mind and body. This may require time and patience on your part, but it is a critical piece. If you allow the child to remove himself before *you* have deemed him calm, your child will not take Stop Everything seriously and it will fail.

- While sitting together the message for the child is, *"I'll wait until you are ready to be with me,"* or "*I see your body isn't ready to ....* (whatever you were doing previously). *I'll wait.*" This emphasizes the importance of them calming themselves and becoming regulated.

Initially, this may take a while until the child realizes that *nothing* is going to happen until s/he calms down his/her body and voice completely and is ready to focus on you again.

- Once calm, be together in silence for a minute, and then try resume what you had been doing together prior to the dysregulation.
- **Note**—do not try to resume your joint engagement the second your child is quiet. Wait until your child has demonstrated at least one or two minutes of quiet regulation before getting up. Chances are, if you get up too quickly, your child will revert back to the dysregulated state he was in before. If you find this is the case, repeat the Stop Everything technique of sitting quietly together. Use this technique as often as necessary. If the child senses that you are serious about this and that really *nothing* is going to happen until he can show you that he is ready to be with you (is focused and willing to resume the activity with you as the leader), he will comply. He has no other choice if you follow this regime.
- Remember, you are the parent, so act and speak with authority. When your child is out of control, your child needs to sense that you are the boss, and what you say goes. This will teach her that you demand respect, and what a great lesson it is! (Again, if your child is a danger to themselves or others, I recommend that you seek professional help.)

Ingredient Number 3: Use an Appropriate Communication Style

Imperative vs. Declarative Language

Doing actions together, or co-regulating, is not enough without good communication. True connections are made on an emotional level. We must help our children with autism make use of the social/emotional world around them. This is a critical step in The Social Diet. The way we do this is to understand how we can optimize our own communication style in order to form deeper connections with our children. The only way that humans have ever been able to learn from one another and form meaningful relationships is through communicating. Communication is everything. It encompasses both our verbal and non-verbal behavior. Without it, we would be lost. It is the foundation of the human story.

Despite how powerful and influential communication is, most of us go through life never stopping to think about it. We are unaware of how our communication affects our own behavior and that of our children. What we say and how we say something, and even what we don't say, are all powerful teaching tools that affect what we learn, how we learn, and what others learn from us. Being a Sociolinguist by education and nature, I have learned that how people use communication can have profound effects on learning, relationship building, and behavioral outcomes. The proverb "*It's not what you say, but how you say it*" is very true.

The way someone speaks– their tone, pitch, cadence, volume, body language, and facial expressions-- all carry meaning. For example, you can say, “I love you” to someone, but if you are shouting these words in a cruel tone, chances are that your message will *not* be received as genuine. Compare this to someone whispering “I love you” to you while handing you a flower. The words can be identical, but the way they are said, and the environment in which you find yourself makes all the difference to the reception and outcome of the communication.

Believe it or not, only 15% of communication is made of words or verbal language. Roughly 85% of our communication is non-verbal. “A picture is worth 1,000 words” is not just a saying! The challenge with individuals with autism is that not only do they struggle with *verbal* communication, they typically do not use or understand societal *non-verbal* components of communication. Even in the best-case scenario, where a non-NT child has strong verbal skills, chances are he or she still isn’t easily able to naturally pick-up on the much larger, non-verbal pieces which form our daily lives. This puts even the best of speakers at a significant disadvantage. It is a generally known fact that individuals with autism have a difficult time perceiving social contextual clues.

You might be aware that those on the spectrum interpret things literally. What they hear is what they expect to happen. This is because they do not perceive the nuances which come with spoken language. For example, if someone said, “You look very pretty” but gave you a look of disgust as they said it, you would know that the person was not sincere. In this instance, even though the words say something, the body language, face, and tone send another message. If we don't have communication challenges, we can pick up on this very easily and understand that the speaker is being sarcastic. This is commonly not the case for the population with ASD and other neurological disorders with processing delays. Unless we work specifically on a curriculum like The Social Diet which addresses this issue, children will not be able to understand the meaning behind the words. They will lose out on the ultimate function of what it means to be human—the ability to experience our social/emotional world together. Being aware of your current style and choosing an appropriate communication style is our teaching tool toward a more connected life. This ingredient of The Social Diet aims to empower you and give you the tools you will need to connect with those you love on a deeper level.

Becoming Aware of Your Communication - The Use of Physical Space

As a trained Sociolinguist, the first thing I do when go into a home or school is to look at communication skills and techniques. This includes the verbal and non-verbal behavior of all the participants, especially the adults in charge. It also includes the actual physical space. How people use physical space is meaningful. It can often determine whether, or not, the social interactions will be successful or not. Adults cannot lead a child with the intent in keeping a social connection, if the child is not physically close, or if the child's body is not oriented toward them.

So, the first place to start when you look at your own communication is to begin by looking at how you and your child are interacting in the physical space.

Questions I suggest you ask yourself:

- Where is the child in relation to myself?
- How close or how far apart are we to one other?
- How are we sharing our space? Are we facing each other, or is the child's back to me?
- Am I the most important thing to the child or is she distracted by something or someone else? (Take away anything that distracts from you being the focus.)
- Are their body, face, and feet all oriented to face me? Are mine oriented towards them?

The answers to the above questions may vary, but there are certain components for which you will want to search, in order to be a successful social partner. First, again, it is important that you and the child are within arm's reach of one another. The closer you are to the child the more effective your verbal and non-verbal behavior become. If the child is not in a physical position to look at you, he will not be able to pick up your non-verbal communication. This is the part we want to enhance the most, so it is imperative that the child's body orientation is one that aligns with yours, with both face and feet pointed towards you. I find it best when you and your child are at a 45-degree angle or right across from each other. This angle is conducive to sharing your faces but also sharing your physical space.

Your Communication Style

Once you have a look at the use of the physical space, you want to investigate the communication itself.

Further questions to ask yourself:

- What does my communication style look like?
- Am I talking/lecturing too much? Is the child talking too much?
- How am I using non-verbal communication? Examine your tone, volume, pitch, facial expressions, facial gazes, and body posture to help enhance the social and emotional connection with each other.
- What might I need to do or say differently, so my guidance becomes the most salient feature for the child?

Don't Tell Your Child What To Do:

Imperative vs. Declarative Language.

We live in a culture where we love to tell our children what to do. "Put on your shoes." "Go get dressed." "Take a shower." "Do your homework." We equally spend our time telling them what not to do. "Don't touch your sister." "Don't say that." "Don't bother me." We are so busy telling our kids what or what not to do that this becomes practically *all* we do. This kind of language style is called imperative language. It is used so much because it is efficient and quick in many situations. The problem is that it's not conducive to emotional or social sharing. It doesn't work effectively with strong willed children and works even less with children who are non-neurotypical in any way. Much frustration can happen from a parent who uses this style, and expects rote obedience, immediate compliance, and does not get it from their child.

An imperative style of communication is either an imperative (a command) as in the above examples, ("Go get dressed!"), but it can also occur in the form of questions. We use imperative language when we want the listener to do comply by creating answers to questions like, "What time is it?","What is your name?", "How many states are there in the United States?" All questions to which there is a specific "right" or "wrong" answer fall under imperative language.

In my experience, imperative language is used more than 80% in classroom and home environments. Why does this matter? The problem is that when you use an imperative form of communication you are *not* sharing each other's state of minds-- perceptions, experiences, attitudes, and opinions. Imperative language is static. It gives a command and requires a rote response or action. There does not need to be any connection or reasoning. With imperative language there is no decision-making happening, no need to be flexible, no need to socially relate to the person you are talking to. You just need to do what the person is telling you to do, or not.

When we have children on the spectrum who grow up with the adults in their lives using almost exclusively imperative language, the child's receptive and expressive language repertoire becomes extremely narrow. Instead of using a communication style which allows us to share our thoughts and feelings with our children, they are taught, albeit indirectly, that the purpose of language serves two basic functions. The first is to get our own needs and wants met, and the other is to do, or not do, what other people want of us. Communication should encompass so much more than this narrow function! This is especially true if we want to teach our kids about the social/emotional world. In order to do this important thing, we need a communication style which supports this kind of learning. We need a means to express and share the experience we have together.

Let us examine this point more closely. If someone tells you what or what not to do, you might not like it or agree with it, but you don't have to think about it. As an example: “Drink your milk.” The speaker cares about only one thing, that you drink your milk. They are not concerned with what you *think* about it, they just want you to do it. You become a *good* person if you comply and do it or become a *bad* person if you don’t. The focus and the purpose become all about the doing or not doing.

Here is the catch, and the blind spot for most parents and educators. If you suffer from autism, being able to follow directions, although very important in early stages of life, becomes the perpetual goal, at the expense of your child becoming more of a creative, flexible, social, and eventually independent thinker. Rote obedience might turn your child into a compliant child, which is a necessary first step. However, you do not need to partake in this direct method. Compliance is not enough when learning how to engage in the social world.

Let’s think back to the letter my son wrote to me for Valentine’s Day. He could have never written such a heartfelt letter to me if he had spent the elementary years of his life following a rote curriculum of only answering adult questions and following rote instructions. In order for him to be able to have original thoughts and initiate and be motivated to write me a love letter on his own, and not as an assignment, he needed to spend hundreds of hours, over years, in an enriching, communicative, social and loving environments.

Using Declarative Language- Sharing the Social World Together

The communication style that is needed to teach a social curriculum, such as The Social Diet, is called *declarative* language. Think of declarative language as what you do when you talk to yourself, only you do it out loud. With a declarative style you do just that—you *declare* what is going on for you. This includes sharing your thoughts on what's going on in the immediate social world. It includes giving your opinion, sharing how you feel, or noticing something that is going on in the moment. As long as you are not telling someone to do something, or asking a question to get a specific answer, you are using declarative language.

For example, you could say something like, "I am ready. I have my shoes on." You are not telling the child what to do, as in "Go get your shoes," but you are stating what is happening for you. By choosing a declarative statement you afford the child the opportunity to not only model after you (an important developmental milestone), but also you give your child the opportunity to learn what is important and salient for you. You become the focus, not the child.

You want your child to focus on what you are *doing*. While you are declaring, "I am ready, I have my shoes on," you are allowing the child to learn what is going on in your experience and think of what needs to occur in their own experience. This is a critical step if we want to teach empathy. It also allows a venue for your child to become aware of the subjective world through your eyes. How else will they be able to one day form their own appropriate perceptions, attitudes or viewpoints? Declarative language is the only way to tap into their higher-thinking cognitive processes.

Putting Declarative Language Into Practice

The first step in using declarative language for yourself is to take notice of how you communicate. Ideally, you want to use declarative language 80 percent of the time and an imperative style no more than 20 percent. (Another 80/20 rule). This can be difficult at first. Intellectually, we may understand the need for declarative language, but it is hard to put this into practice. Nevertheless, we must stop the urge to constantly tell our children what to do. I suggest making lots of "I" statements. This means that you can begin by stating something about how you are feeling or what you are thinking. "I am thinking we can go to the park today, it's so nice out." "I bet it's going to rain. I can see big clouds in the sky." "I wonder what Daddy would like?" Another strategy is to begin your statements with "Let's…" "Let's go to the store for some milk." "Let's make a birthday cake for your teacher." This emphasizes doing something together. It is not an order. It is communicating together, more like and invitation.

Once you put your thought or statement out there-- "I am ready, I have my shoes on"-- you want to make sure the child takes notice. Because autism is a spectrum, some children will be able to follow your thoughts and actions with little problem. However, most will not-- they will need your help. Because declarative language is not direct, our children with autism often initially miss the point. This does not mean that we should revert back to telling them what to do. Rather, it means that as the guide you must work harder to make the declarative communication understood. You need to learn to "scaffold."

Scaffolding is giving your children the necessary support needed to learn how to react to declarative language. It does not mean that you compensate or do things for them, it means that you break down the communicative environment in way that is manageable. Your job is to get them to understand your intent without telling them what or what not to do (using and imperative). Think of it as when your child was small, that you would cut up their food for them in order to better facilitate their being able to eat. The end result and goal are the same, but you performed additional steps in order to facilitate that result.

Let me demonstrate by using my original declarative statement, "I am ready, I have my shoes on." Ideally, you want the child to look at your feet, see your shoes on, take in the message and go and put on his shoes, all without you having to say or do anything more. This is unlikely to happen initially, with any child, and much less likely with a non-NT child. Therefore, the next step of scaffolding might be that you look deliberately at your feet, then at his feet and repeat, "I am ready. I have my shoes on." If that doesn't work, then we scaffold some more. Look at his feet and then move your gaze and body in the direction of his shoes and say, "I see your shoes." The trick here is not to use an imperative.

When you say, "I see your shoes," you are not saying "Go get your shoes." You might think that this is the same thing, but it is not. When you say "I," you are telling your child about what is going on for you. You want him to be able to make the inference of "Okay, I see Mom has her shoes on, I guess I need to go get mine." Making inferences is such a critical step in higher-level developmental thinking. If you simply tell him what to do, he doesn't have to do the hard work of figuring it out for himself. You've done the thinking for him!

Examples of Imperative Language versus Declarative Language

Imperative Language = **Telling** Someone What to Do or **Asking** a Question

(You have a specific action or answer you are looking for.)

Ex.
Go get your shoes!
Stop talking so loud!
Finish Eating!
What color is this?
Who is the President of the United States?
How many days are there in a week?

Declarative Language = **Stating** What You Are **Noticing** (You are ***inviting*** someone to just take notice in what you are saying)

Ex. I wonder if it's going to rain (while you look up into the cloudy dark sky.)

I have my shoes on (while you look down at your feet and then your child's.)

Boy, I'm really hungry (pause and waiting for them to tell you they are too.)

That dog is so cute! (in hopes that they look over to see what you are looking at.)

I'm going to finish my work and then relax (to model work then play.)

I understand that this may be difficult for a lot of children at first, but you must believe me that when you become skilled at using declarative language, amazing things start to happen! Suddenly you plant the seed for your child that—believe it or not—he *is not* the center of the universe. There are other people in the world, and what they do and how they feel really *does* matter. In order to grow up being able to integrate successfully in a social world, we all have to be able to empathize and understand other people's perspectives. This is a natural stage of child development, but one that can be difficult for children with communicative delays to reach without these techniques to help.

It starts with a simple declarative statement of "I'm folding *my* clothes." Suddenly, you have opened up the event of folding clothes to become an exercise for your child to make inferences, deductions, and take in *your* perspective. Suddenly, you are paving the way for them to think at a higher level and exercise their brain to become more flexible, to problem solve and understand other people's actions and feelings. It is really quite amazing!

Ingredient Number 4: Healthy Inter-dependence before Healthy Independence

No matter where I go in the country, I hear the same thing: "*We want our child to become independent.*" "Independence" seems to be the buzz word of the century for our culture and something we start teaching even the youngest of toddlers—even those with autism. I understand. Who doesn't want their child, especially one with autism to become independent? But, hold on… *not so fast*! We need to stop and think about this in a serious way. This is an area of study which is very misunderstood by parents and professionals. By definition, independence means to be able to do things for oneself. I believe, however, that pushing independence too soon in a child's development is counterproductive and even dangerous for our autism population for two important reasons.

The first reason is that we do not want to emphasize autonomy in a population which is already predisposed to wanting to do things *by themselves*. Individuals with autism or the like need a Social Diet for this very reason. They do not intrinsically know how to do the social piece, no matter how intelligent and autonomous they can be with taking things apart or completing detailed tasks. By allowing them more time doing things *independently* they will never learn how to become socially proficient. We learn how to be social only by being social. This is not intending to create codependency, but an initial interdependency, which can enhance communication skills and the capability to depend on perspectives and ideas beyond their own.

This brings us to the second reason why pushing independence too soon can be detrimental. Learning independence does not happen in a vacuum. Instead, true independence is a learned behavior. Before learning how to be independent, you first have to spend hours and hours, if not years and years being an active co-participator alongside more seasoned social partners who are experienced in the social world. My definition of independence is probably much broader than most parents, or professionals.

To me, becoming independent means being able to think through issues, problem solve, figure out what is going on in the environment, and come up with more than one solution. It also means having the ability to do this within an appropriate social setting. To me, being independent is much more than learning how to make your bed, or brush your teeth by yourself, or make a sandwich, or drive. Although these are necessary skills, they are what are known as the *hard skills* and will not give children the ability to think on their feet, nor be able to find solutions to what life might throw their way. I think a lot of us fail to recognize this. Most people are under the assumption that if we can get the child to do things on his own, he will then magically become independent. This is simply not true.

If we agree that autism is a processing disorder, it is extremely unlikely that any pre-school or elementary age child with autism is developmentally ready to become an independent thinker. They do not yet have the tools which they need to become dynamic thinkers who can problem-solve, or think flexibly. How can you say someone is ready to become independent, when they don't have the social/emotional foundations to do so? Just because we want them to be independent does not mean they can skip the rudimentary and foundational skills it takes to eventually become independent.

In order for the process of The Social Diet to be successful, the parent or adult needs to set up the environmental interactions where the child is an active co-participator. The Senior Partner cannot do his job without a child partner. Nor can the child do his job without you.

Co-Regulation-

Working Together As a Team

Joining together or working as a team can also be called co-regulation. To co-regulate means that each person is able to regulate his own actions and thoughts to compliment those of his/her communication partner. Both of you are need to be in sync. The Social Diet is all about the ability to co-regulate, at least at the basic level. Being self-regulated means that a person has the ability to think and act appropriately. It refers to both the physical and emotional aspects of a person. Self-regulation is extremely hard for our children with autism. It involves the ability to monitor and manage one's emotions. It also means being able to read the emotions of others and to remain calm, flexible, and deal with challenges in a manageable way. The opposite of self-regulation is dysregulation. Often, we see children with autism who are dysregulated. They are easily frustrated when things do not go their way and are not able to deal well in the face of uncertainty. The Social Diet recognizes how important it is to be able to manage one's actions and thoughts appropriately. Like with independence, children cannot learn how to self-regulate until they have spent enough time co-regulating with a person who is self-regulated.

There is no possible way that your child can be successful in relationships if he has not spent enough time as a willing co-regulator. When you teach your child to co-regulate with you, you are working on social awareness. To be able to co-regulate means having the ability to co-exist with your partner while interacting together. It means being able to do things together as a team. As a team, each of your roles is critical. They are symbiotic. I can't do my job if my child isn't actively doing his. We are working together. Co-regulation is the moment-by-moment changes in the environment that demand our attention. So, if I do something differently, you, as my partner, need to pay attention to that and be able to change what you are doing to keep the flow of our interaction together.

A simple example of co-regulation is tossing a ball back and forth together. In order for each partner to catch the ball in turn, partner A has to be aware of where partner B is. Several things have to be *aligned,* such as each person's physical space, the velocity of the ball, the ability of each partner to catch and throw a ball, and the size of the ball. All these factors play a role, if the repeated throwing and catching is going to be successful. If one throws the ball too far to the left, that forces the partner to move to be able to catch. Once she catches it, that partner has to readjust position to realign with her partner. Without this kind of awareness, your ball throwing activity could be unsuccessful. It often is, when learning how to throw and catch! There is more to it than meets the eye.

The example of the ball toss can be used as a metaphor for life. You have to be attuned with your partner and have the ability to align and to readjust as the environment and social context change. Co-regulation gives our children the practice they need to do this important skill.

How do I Teach Co-Regulation?

Co-regulating is very natural for kids without neurotypical delays. They innately know how to join in socially, and often without effort. Our children with social challenges, though, have to be explicitly shown how to do this. The trick is not to have to "tell" them what to do. The whole point of true co-regulation is having the ability to be aware of your partner without verbal communication. I will offer optimal ways of communicating in the next section. For now, it suffices to say that if you need to tell the child every step of what you want, he or she is not co-regulating. The child might be complying but not co-regulating in a natural way. It is your job to set up a non-verbal environment in such a way that the child can follow along without having to use explicit words.

Giver-Putter Exercise

The rudimentary steps to co-regulation involve doing simple, non-verbal, back and forth actions such as a ball toss (as in the above example) or what I call the "Giver to Putter" actions[7]. The "Giver to Putter" exercise is one way to practice co-regulation in its simplest form. The Parent or adult is the "Giver" and the child is the "Putter."

The Giver gives something to the Putter and the Putter puts it away. Some activities that come to mind are putting silverware or dishes away. Putting books on a bookshelf or cleaning up toys are other ideas. The important thing here is that the adult starts the action and the child completes the action. Just a simple "my turn, then your turn" is what you are after. Be careful, however, of your pace. The whole idea is for the child to become calm and to match your emotional state. This is not a time to rev things up so it becomes too quick or chaotic. You want your actions to be slow and deliberate. You want to see if your child can stay with you. If you change something up, you want your child to notice the change and adjust his or her actions and thinking accordingly.

So, for example, if you give the child some spoons to put away, and suddenly you change it up and give her a fork, you want the child to notice this change, and to alter what needs to be done. The

---

[7] I borrowed this from my RDI colleague Amy Cameron's "Blitzing" activity.

fork would not go with the spoons, but with the other forks. By changing things up slightly, you are teaching the child to pay attention, because at any given moment something might be different. Adding variation is a necessary component to understanding that things in life might be patterned, but things do change, and change is not bad. Their job is to pay attention and be able to adapt.

If the child is calm and regulated, then you can switch roles. The child can be the Giver and you can become the Putter. Be careful though-- do not allow your child to become dysregulated. If your child cannot handle being the Giver calmly, revert back to you leading. There will be other times to progress to switching roles.

Action/Counteraction Technique

Another way to teach co-regulation is by using an Action/Counteraction technique, which can be used once the Giver/Putter exercises have been mastered. In Action/Counter Action, the Senior Partner does an action and the child does a counteraction in response. Ideas that come to mind are sweeper/dustpan, spray cleaner/wiper, or you start cleaning up and the child joins in. Here the guide starts an action, and without being told what to do, the child is able to pay attention and add an action that is appropriate.

Four More Co-regulation Techniques

Not every child is able to do the above techniques at first. Your child may need more support. Do not think this is a failure, just a developmental stage which you are continuing to encourage. Below I introduce more basic techniques which you can use to teach co-regulation. There are four basic ways.

1) Hand over Hand

The first is Hand over Hand. This is where the guide and the child do the same action hand over hand, with the adult leading. You can stir together, pour together, jump together-- any action is acceptable, as long as you do it at the same time and in the same way. Picking up the same toy or book together and putting it away would also constitute a Hand over Hand technique.

2) My Turn, Your Turn

The second way to teach co-regulation is by using the My Turn, Your Turn technique. Here, the adult and the child do the same action, but one right after the other. So, you might stir something, and then it's the child's turn. As always, it is important that the child remains regulated when it is their turn. By definition, you want the child to look to you for information, and be able to mirror you. There is always a connection between the adult and the child, even when it's the other person's turn for action. You want to make sure that you are completely present for one another. If your child somehow becomes silly or wants to take control, this is not co-regulation.

When and if this happens, it is a signal for the Parent that your child might not be ready to take a turn. If this is the case, go back to *Hand Over Hand* actions. Once the child is back with you, you can try again.

1) Synchronized Actions with Separate Tools

This third way to co-regulate is much like the Hand Over Hand technique. In addition to doing something together, you are each responsible for your own tools. *Synchronized Actions with Separate Tools* means that the Senior Partner has his own set of tools, and so does the child. So, for example if you are making pudding and stirring, you each have your own spoon and your own bowl. Here, you would stir the same way at the same time with your own tools. You can see that this adds a little more responsibility for the child. As mentioned above, not all kids will be able to do this and remain regulated. If this is the case, you may want to stick with only the Hand over Hand or the My Turn Your Turn techniques until your child can progress.

2) One Action after Another with Separate Tools

This fourth technique demands even more of the child's focus and awareness. If your child has demonstrated proficiency in the other three techniques, you can then try this last step. In *One Action after Another with Separate Tools,* the parent does something using his own tools and then the child is expected to follow suit. The two of you are successful if your actions remain fluid and your emotional state remains connected. If we keep with the same example of stirring the pudding, the Sr. Partner would stir first and then the child would be given a turn. Then back to the adult and then the child.

It is important for the parent to add variations to the actions, for reasons we mentioned above. If things remain too rote, it can get boring for both of you and most likely the child will let you know. Remember, it's not just what you are doing, but how you are doing it that may keep the child interested in this game. Look to the child's behavior as clues. A child will tell you how well you are doing based on his or her ability and motivation to stay connected with you.

Diagram 1
4 Ways to do an Action Together (Co-Regulation)

1) Hand Over Hand	**2) My Turn, Your Turn**
Parent and child do the same action hand over hand with the adult leading. **Example 1:** Both of you stir some pudding in one bowl with the one spoon. **Example 2:** You are both sweeping at the same time with the same broom.	Parent and child do the same action, but one right after the other. (You take a turn, then the child takes a turn doing the same action, the same way, at the same pace.) **Example 1:** The Parent stirs the pudding using one bowl and one spoon. The child then takes a turn doing what you just did. **Example 2:** The parent sweeps then the child sweeps.

3) Synchronized Actions with Separate Tools	4) Action One After the Other with Separate Tools
Parent and child each have their own tools and they do the action together at the same time. **Example 1:** The Parent has a bowl and a spoon and the child has a bowl and a spoon. Together the parent and child stir at the same time in the same manner, each with their separate bowls. **Example 2:** The guide sweeps into the dustpan as the child is holding it.	Parent and child each have their own tools and do the action one after the other with the adult starting the action. **Example 1:** Parent and child each has a separate bowl and spoon. The parent stirs first and then allows the child to take a turn and stir on his own. **Example 2:** The guide sweeps, then the child picks up the dust with the dustpan.

Ingredient Number 5: Teach Skills Via Relationships:

This is something that most parents and professionals fail to understand. As a field, we are working so hard on getting the child to learn skills, at the expense of spending more time building relationships. The problem is not *what* our children are learning. The problem is *how* they are learning. Hard skills are usually taught in isolation. They mostly require that the child do rote memorization. When you memorize, however, you are not tapping into that part of the brain which promotes life learning and requires using the higher cognitive processing. When you memorize, skills are often forgotten, or not necessarily retrievable in real life circumstances. The kind of knowledge that your child will need for a successful life can only be learned within a social emotional context. The social emotional connections that are established between you and your child will determine whether or not something is learned for good. By you setting up a relationship focused learning environment, your child is more likely to internalize the information given. When you internalize something, you make it your own. When you make it your own, you can retrieve it and apply it to the real world.

The question then becomes, "How does my child learn to internalize information?" The answer, I've found, is by learning skills within a socially based context. The trick is to learn the skills through relationships.

My son and I had a blast learning the alphabet together. All it took was a bit of creativity and the ability to use our relationship as a means to a social end. I had some alphabet carpet squares with a different letter on each square. I would place some carpets squares around the room and together, we would jump from one carpet to the next. I made sure we had lots of fun. I would kneel down to his level, have a huge smile on my face, and with a fun and exciting tone would call out, "Ok, Ylann let's find the letter "Y." I would glance at it without saying a word, look back quickly at him, look at the letter again. My job was to get him socially connected with me before even "doing" anything.

I wanted to reinforce that we are doing this game *together* and enjoying it together. I also wanted him to be able to follow my glance, see me get excited about finding the letter and then see him smile when he found it too. He didn't realize that I was setting up the environment to foster our social connectedness, he just thought he was having fun with Mommy and finding letters. I, however, knew that in this small activity of jumping together, I was working on his ability to follow my thoughts, thinking, and behavior. I did this by using a declarative communication style in a way that would promote his social awareness of both me and his environment. The simple act of me gazing at a letter, and then looking to him, and back to the letter, and then him being able to follow my thoughts, is nothing less than a miracle. I say *miracle* because I know that if my son had the capacity to understand what I was doing without me saying anything and just a body position change on my part (turning my head) looking towards a letter, that mean that he *could perceive what I was thinking.*

Perceiving other peoples' thoughts are critical in typical social emotional development. The ability to understand what someone else might be thinking, without having spoken, starts the seeds toward empathy and caring for others.

In my son's case I started with a verbal statement but coupled it with a non-verbal action- turning my head and eye gaze to the "Y" on the floor, at which point Ylann turned, found the letter "Y" and smiled. As we worked on this more and more, I was able to fade the verbal prompting and just look at a letter and he would know which one I was referring to. We used this technique time and time again, for him to learn other things with me. I remember hiding things in the living room and he having to look at me to figure out where the object was hiding. He learned about my likes and dislikes early on by playing a tasting game together. I sit him next to me and had three foods that I loved, and three foods that I hated. At first I would use some words, but only a few. I might have said, "Mmm! This is so yummy!" It was my physical affect that I wanted him to focus upon. When I liked a food my eyes and face would light up. My tone would be upbeat and my body position inviting. My job here was to make sure he noticed me; I wanted him to be able to transfer what I was thinking and feeling to himself. The words were minimal at first, but my body and face gave the message. I did the same when I didn't like a food. He could tell from my actions and facial expressions that I wanted no part of that food. I made it funny by using a silly voice and saying, "Yuck, yuck this is TERRIBLE!" He would laugh and laugh at me each time I said it. We had so much fun doing so little.

Again, the importance in this activity or social event is not so much learning the names of certain foods, or trying new things to eat. Although that is a desired by-product, the food served as a way to teach him what was going on *for me*- what it was that I thought and felt. In the world of autism where narcissism tends to be king, using a social perspective is the only way to teach our children that yes, we love them, and hanging out with people is way cool! We are social beings that are a part of a community. In caring about community, we learn about caring for others and ourselves in a nurturing healthy way.

Ingredient Number 6: Building Friendships and Community

Why community? My first question is why not community? Think about it. Think about the things that you are most proud of- your achievements your successes your most valued assets in this world and I'm not talking about material assets. Now imagine if you would be able to have gratitude if you did not have people who were supporting you and helping you and loving you every step of the way.

I don't care who you are, or what kind of personality you have. I don't care what disability, gifts, talents, ambitions one has. No one never gets through life on their own. Sure there are people who are introverts. Some might enjoy the company of others but need some time to themselves. Others of us prefer their own company and would rather be by themselves. You might think your child is this way. Others of us have had negative experiences with people and have learned to shut others out. This does not mean that community is not important. This does not mean that you don't need community.

Think about your life. Think about your teachers your parents your neighbors your friends. We all need support. We all need community. Even at the most difficult times our children are there to remind us to reach out and find people that will support us.

What Makes Us Happy: ***Feeding our Human Need***

For those of you who have read anything about the subject of happiness, you know about the following truism. When elders are asked what brought them their biggest joys in life, it is the relationships they had with people. According to the research (and common sense), being with loved ones is the number one ingredient for living longer lives, having better health, and experiencing a more fulfilling and joyful life.

Not spending enough time with family or friends is the number one regret.

The book, "The 5 Secrets You Must Discover Before You Die" by John Izzo is a fabulous reminder of this. Izzo interviewed more than 200 people in senior years of life, from all walks of life. What he found was that relationships with others are what matter most. But why? What is it about being with others that matters more than anything else in life? I turn to human nature for the answer.

Take a moment to think about and truly understand on a deep level that we are all social beings. It is so obvious that we seem to overlook it. Seriously, do you wake up in the morning and say to yourself, "Hey, I am a human being and I have social/emotional needs that need to be fed today?"

If you want to incorporate The Social Diet into your life you must think about and live in a way that puts your human needs first. This is extremely important. This can be difficult since we live in a culture that doesn't value this. We think we are being selfish or that we don't have time to take care of ourselves. Think again. You don't have time *not* to take care of yourself. You need to nourish yourself so you can nourish your child(ren).

If you are a parent or a role model for others, I strongly encourage you to adopt this way of thinking and living. You are the most important role model for your children. When your children are young, your main job is *not* to teach them their ABC's or how to count. As a parent your main and most important job is to feed your children the quintessential social/emotional diet they need to thrive in their lives.

If our human needs are not met, we will suffer and we will feel pain. It's that simple. We might not think we are suffering but on some level we are. It might come out in our personal relationships, (the one with ourselves or those closest to us). It might pop up in our work environment or where we spend most of our time. Worse yet, it may show up in our relationship we have with our children. We don't want this.

We may be able to fool ourselves intellectually and come up with all the reasons why we are fine. A lot of us are not even aware because we are so busy taking care of things "less important" than ourselves. But the reality is that our hearts and our bodies know differently. If our human need of having loving people in our lives are not being met on a daily basis, we are out of balance and will pay the price in some way or another. We cannot have a well-balanced, healthy and joyful life without others in it.

For the reasons above, (and everything else you have read so far), I have come up with The Social Diet Wheel of Balance and Health.

The Social Diet®

Wheel of Balance and Health for Parents/Caregivers

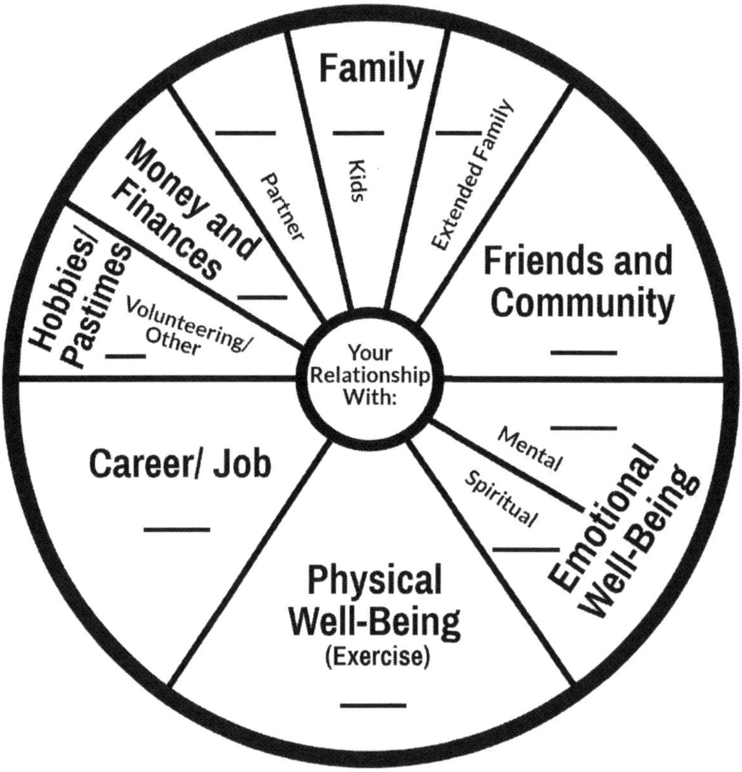

On a scale from 1-10, with one being not strong to ten being extremely strong, what number would you put for each of these ten categories? Add that number together and divide by ten. What is your final score? How in balance are you?

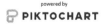

powered by PIKTOCHART

www.TheSocialDiet.net

Infographic by Allie Datz created with Piktochart

The Social Diet®

Wheel of Balance and Health for Children

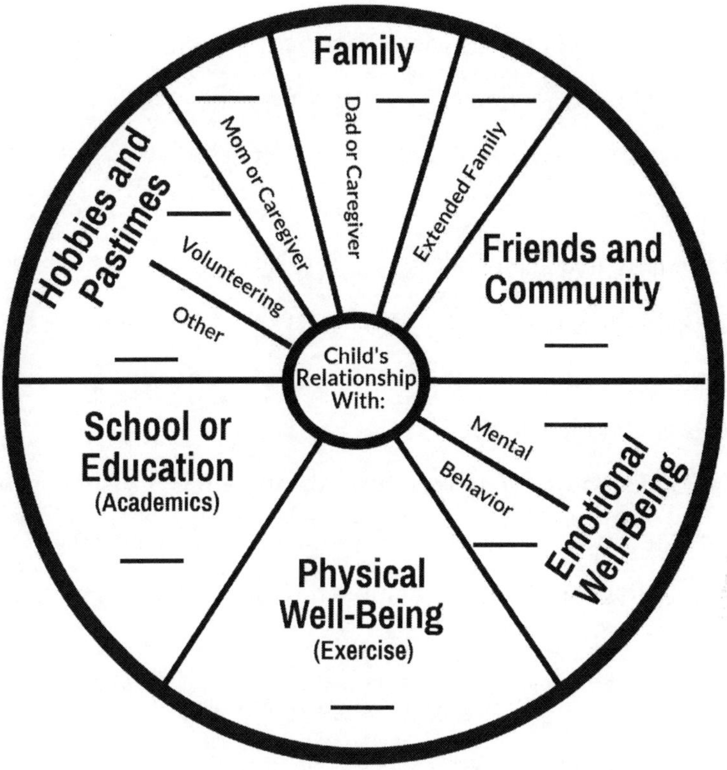

On a scale from 1-10, with one being not strong to ten being extremely strong, what number would you put for each of these ten categories? Add that number together and divide by ten. What is your final score? How in balance are you?

www.TheSocialDiet.net

Infographic by Allie Datz created with Piktochart

The Social Diet Wheel of Balance and Health is a tool which parents/caregivers can use for themselves, as well as for their children. I have designed the one wheel for the adults in your child's life and one for your children. If you have a partner each one of you need to have your own wheel, as does each child. Couples, you do not fill this out together, however you can help guide your child through it if needed. The purpose of the wheel is to get some quick feedback in order to see which areas in your life flow and what areas of life may need some attention. It is by no means an exhaustive list of all the things that make up your life. You are free to add your own categories and sub-categories as you see fit, but hopefully it is a good general use tool.

Notice that some of areas are sub-divided. This is the case for the Family section, for example. I divided this piece up, so as to account for the different kind of relationships which you may exhibit with different members of your family. For example, the score which you might give your spouse or significant other could be very be different than the one you give to your child.

How to Rate Yourself

Rate yourself in each category, using a scale of 1-10 where 1 represents the weakest mark (meaning this area is practically nonexistent for you) to 10, which represents an extremely strong score (meaning that things in this area couldn't be better). You can think of these numbers as percentage scores. For example, if you give yourself a rating of 8 in an area, that number would correspond to 80%. If your child is old enough and capable enough, have him or her fill out the Child Wheel in the same fashion. (This can be a good learning opportunity for both of you. Once your child has completed the wheel, it lends itself to a rich follow-up discussion.) If your child is too young, or not capable of understanding the meaning of the wheel, score their wheel for them in terms of how you see them. This can be a real eye opener.

Picture the wheel diagram as a bike wheel. The wheel is a visual for how well your life is running. If you have a balanced wheel that performs at its maximum potential, all your areas of life would be at a ten. This score signifies that you are at 100% of where you want to be, and you are rolling effortlessly in your life. Be honest with your scores; no one has to see this chart, but you.

The Wheel is Fluid

This wheel is meant to be a fluid diagram. The scores you give yourself can change at any given moment. That is the beauty of it—the wheel is meant to represent the fluidity of life. One minute, you might feel at an all-time high, and you give yourself a nine or a 10; yet, within a moment's time, something may change and you no longer feel that way. I suggest filling out your wheel in the evening, to get an average score for that day.

You may choose to fill out your Wheel each day, each week or each month. I recommend doing it at least one time a week, for 12 weeks. That will give you enough time to see the patterns that are developing.

I use this wheel with the young people and families whom I help, and have learned: this simple exercise is surprisingly difficult! Self-reflection is not for the faint of heart. It takes courage, vulnerability, commitment, and a love of yourself to commit to doing this self-evaluation on a regular basis, and to act upon what you see. There is no judgment whatsoever here, but if this exercise frightens you, ask yourself *why* and get the support you need to be able to face your fears. No healthy progress can be made if you are afraid to look at reflection in the mirror.

It takes a brave and courageous person to look at these numbers and take action if you do not like what you see, or how you feel. I encourage all of you who have a score below 8 in any of the categories to step forward and tackle these strategies head on. When you do, I promise, as you and your child progress in The Social Diet, you will live an amazing life and become that amazing person (mother, father, aunt, uncle, neighbor, employee, etc.) you were born to be. Our happiest moments in life (and even our saddest) are the most meaningful and heartfelt when we are able to connect with others. This is why we have traditions and rituals, weddings, births, and graduations—there are reasons we invite our favorite people to witness and celebrate our milestones with us. I recently lost one of my closest friends, Gaye. Right after, she suddenly passed away. My extended family and I were about to embark on a trip to celebrate our parents 60th wedding anniversary. Instead of being excited about the imminent trip to Tuscany, I was distracted by my grief, and my friend's memorial service. I thought, "I hope I don't miss Gaye's celebration of life event." I felt I needed to be there, even more than I needed to be in Europe. You see, I needed to surround myself with others who had known Gaye and who had loved her just as much as I did. It is much more than simply "paying respects." Mourners need to grieve, and the natural, needed, and heathy way for this grieving process to happen is to share the experience. Humans have an unequivocal need to be with others. To take this away or think that this is not true, robs us of what makes us human. We are not and never were meant to go through life alone.

Let me be crystal clear here: no one "thing" out there will earn you, your child, or your family a life filled with authentic joy, love and peace other than the love you have for yourself first and secondly the love you share for and with those around you. Things do not and cannot bring anyone a meaningful, purposeful life, where true happiness or contentment can be found. Only relationships do. Happiness is designed to be experienced and shared.

We owe it to ourselves and our children and our children's children to do the hard, courageous work it takes to become a happier, healthier more giving human being.

What does it mean to be Successful?

Let's be clear here about what it means by "being successful" or "having success." I think this culture has a different definition than what The Social Diet® calls successful. In our American culture, I believe we associate success with monetary status and a higher perceived social standing in life. While these might indeed denote success, this kind of success is *not* what I am aspiring to instill in your child through the techniques in this book. The type of success that most people talk about can be, and usually is, temporary, and dependent on outside factors. If you have a good fiscal year, you become successful, if you buy an expensive car and live in a posh neighborhood, people call you successful. This sort of success can be fleeting.

To me, the above does not denote success. This denotes a successful *financial* person. If you are good at sales, this makes you a good *sales* person. You are good at your job but being good at your job to me does not necessarily mean that you are a successful *person*. We have many students who have not completed school, in one way or another, and yet they may have the kind of success that Harvard grads may never have.

The kind of success I want for your child is not reliant on outside factors, other job environments, and not on any acquired skill. The kind of success is one which is balanced, thoughtful, caring, giving, happy and alive.

I know I'm asking for a lot. This sort of success is difficult to attain for any adult, even those who are neurotypical in every way, and have had the kindest possible upbringing with every advantage life can afford. But, like with all goals, if I don't ask for it, if I don't aspire to it, if I can't see it, envision it, and feel it, it will not happen. We need to realize that time spent on outside endeavors do not necessarily mean you lead a full, happy life. We must change our priorities as families and redefine what it means to be successful in our homes and communities.

Successful or not Successful?

I have a client with Asperger's who is 29 years old, and who lives on his own and has a full-time job with a computer company. How many of us would love to have our son's reach these good goals? All, of course. But this *is all* that he has. He has a job, he has an apartment, and he is very lucky that he has a loving family. But, is he successful? Yes, in two areas of his life. He has a job, and he can pay for his apartment and living expenses. Does he have friends? *No*. Does he go out and just have fun- either catch a movie, dinner, go to a community event? *No*. Does he have a pet to take care of, or a person other than his colleagues that he talks to? *No*. Does he go out to parties, date, socialize? *No*. Here is a smart, articulate, young man who has a great sense of humor, yet is he successful?

That depends on your definition.

To me he has skills which allow him to have a job, which makes him enough money to live independently. However, skills and money does not a full life make. As charming as I find this young man, (and I really do care for him and believe he has a lot to offer in this world,) he is not connected to other human beings. He is missing this critical piece.

Can we have a successful life without being connected? If the answer is no, (and I posit that it is) then why are we allowing our children and families, to spend most of our waking hours in environments which do not foster connected living? Why do we spend most of our time in school acquiring information and skills? Why is this? I will tell you why. We as a society have lost sight of the most important thing we have, both to offer and to gain: ourselves and each other. If we spent half as much time on learning how important it is to be connected rather than what we need to do to learn how to make money, we would live in a completely different world.

Finding Friends and Community in Your Busy Schedule

The majority of parents have to work to make ends meet. This means that parents have less time and energy to spend engaging with their children. Most of us, especially if you're a single parent (as I am,) you will need outside help and support. We cannot raise a child alone, nor should we expect to be able to do so. The benefits of having a "team" whom you can count is an essential piece of The Social Diet. While kids need consistency in caretakers, they also need exposure to many different people from different backgrounds so that they have opportunities to engage with new people on a frequent basis. The more people who are in your life and your community, the better for you and your kids.

What if you don't have any friends or any community? What should you do? Go find them! Oftentimes friends do not just show up in our lives and we don't just fall into community. Relationships take time and they take effort. Having a non-neurotypical child can be isolating, emotionally and socially, not just for the child, but for their caretakers as well.

Think about all of the communities to which you might already belong, and list them. In order to build friendships and community, you have to put yourself in specific places repeatedly. So, let's say you went to the playground and you met some nice people. The next time you go to the playground, you meet other people, and the third time, more people. You politely nod to the other parents, and go back to being with your own child(ren). This is not bad, and it is pretty typical. However, you can be a little more proactive, and make a trip to the park your quest to find other parents/caregivers with whom you might strike up a conversation. Tell them about yourself. Ask them about their lives and make some comments about their children. If you feel some positive feedback from them, ask them when they typically come to the park. Tell them when you like to go. If you really feel a rapport be bold and ask for their number so that maybe you could text them next time you plan on coming out and you could meet each other. Sometimes, after being isolated for a while, parents and caretakers have to relearn the same friendship and communication skills that we are trying to encourage our children to learn!

If you're already part of a community at a playgroup or parent's group, perhaps it would be OK to get their number, so you could maybe text them and meet each other the next day, or the following week. It's really not that hard to do, if you remember that it is so important and necessary that your child spends time with other kids and adults. Remember you are helping others out by making the first move. Other parents and caregivers who go to the playground with a child often like to meet other adults. The key here is not simply to strike up a conversation with the other parent only, although that may be nice too. You also want to engage both the adult and the child so that a potential friendship can develop with the entire family. Then remember to follow up with a concrete plan.

I have used this technique many times, and it's a great way to meet people and children. I often walk up to strangers and strike up a conversation. In more than 95% of the time, the other person appreciates it because they, too, were there own their own. It's easier than it seems, and with practice, the easier it gets. All it takes really is a smile and say, "Hello, how are you today?" If you have an opened mind, and a giving heart, they will pick up on it and will want to get to know you as well.

Often, other families, especially other parents of special needs children, will not make the first move. Push yourself to do so. When my children were young, I would find myself on the lookout for potential playmates. If there were kind parents and children, I made it a point to go up to them and start a conversation. Before leaving I would say, "Your kids are so great, and they seem to get along well with mine. Do you mind if I take down your number, so we can meet up again?" They all said, "Yes," and I made sure to call within the next couple of days so they wouldn't forget who I was or why I was calling. When my kids were small, I would invite their classmates over as well. It wasn't as critical for my daughter, but my son needed as much practice as he could get with other kids. The more opportunities he had to learn how to play with kids, the better. I couldn't leave children playing by themselves because that would mean that they probably wouldn't stay together as my son didn't have the tools he needed to sustain the interaction back then. He had not yet progressed from what is called “Side Along” play in child development- playing nearby a friend, but not necessarily with them. So, a play date for my son meant that I was “On.” I didn’t let them do anything electronic before they were 12, because I wanted to foster creative play together. I found fun things that kids typically like to do and gave them the support they needed to keep it positive and fun. It did my heart good to see my son play with others. It still does.

Asking people for support can also be positive way to find community and maintain friendships. When you ask someone for a help, chances are that they want to be there for you and help you and your child. Although we don’t talk about it, asking for help from others puts both you and those you ask in a special category. We don’t ask just anyone for support. We ask those whom we know we can count on, and whom we perceive to be good people. On an unconscious level, this means that you value them, and trust them to show up for you and your family. This is a select group of people. In return, when the time comes that they might need a hand, they will be more open to asking you. By helping each other out in times of need, your relationship becomes closer and more personal—this is what friendship is, and what we are trying to teach our children. It gives you opportunities to share new experiences with them that otherwise you might never have shared. The more you share with others, the more open you are, the richer your experiences together become. So next time you hesitate about asking someone for a favor, think again. You might just meet your new best friend.

I often here parents say, "But I don't have the time, (to meet other people)". To that, I say "You cannot afford not to have the time." For the sake of your child's ability to communicate with others in their adulthood, you must model how to become a good friend, and how to communicate with your own peers. In order to help your child to learn how to become a part of a healthy, vibrant community, you must pattern those same steps, so they can learn from your example. Those families who thrive the most are the ones who have a strong connection to their friends and communities.

Questions to think about:

- How comfortable are you with asking people for help? Why or why not?
- Think about what you would say or do if someone you knew asked you for help?
- Would you do it willingly? Why or why not?
- Do your responses to the last question help you to understand that most people will gladly give of their time if you simply ask them?

List as many people as you can in your inner circle. These are the people who are closest to you and would most likely to offer their help and support:

1.

2.

3.

4.

5.

Now list as many people as you can who you might be able to count on if you needed help or support. (These people are not in your inner circle, but you would still feel comfortable reaching out to them if you needed to):

1.

2.

3.

4.

5.

List other people who might be available to lend you a helping hand, if paid for services:

1.

2.

3.

4.

5.

How difficult was it to come up with people in each of the categories?

What steps could you take to find more people to become a part of your team?

1.

2.

3.

4.

5.

Ingredient Number 7: Modeling Love, Respect, and Altruism

What are Human Beings' Most Basic Needs?

We tend to think that since we are human beings with social and emotional needs, we know intrinsically what these needs are. I would venture to say, however, that while the majority of us might be able to name two or three of our basic needs, we probably cannot name the top six. Before reading further, I'd like you to try to think about what these basic social and emotional needs might be.

(The answer is right below so don't look ahead before thinking about it. No cheating!)

Before investigating how to parent in an empowering way, I would first like to frame these questions from the macro perspective: *What is it that all human beings need to feel whole? And what can I do as a parent to make sure that I am giving this to my child?* There are certain basic needs which all people share, no matter where they live, how they live, or how rich or poor an individual might be.

All humans share the following needs. Without them we can not live a life of balance.

1. We need to feel loved by others.
2. We need to feel understood.
3. We need to feel accepted and that we belong—that we are a part of something that is bigger than ourselves.
4. We need to feel safe.

5. We need to feel certainty—that on some level we have some level of control of how we like to organize our day, schedules, and routines.

6. We need novelty in order to keep growing as people. Although the last two needs might not directly be linked to needing be with others, our experiences will always be richer with the presence of others.

It would be important for all people to understand this, especially those of us who are parents and raising the next generation of our human species. I wonder how many of us parents spend time thinking, understanding and educating ourselves about how to raise a socially emotionally, well-balanced child, who is loving? How many of us examine how to raise our children, so that they might grow up feeling joy, seeing the goodness in others, and possess a genuine love for their fellow man and for themselves? No doubt, this is what every parent should want, and we want to be deliberate and thoughtful at how this could become your primary goal as a parent.

It is important for all people to understand these basic necessities to progression and growth, to become whole, complete, and productive individuals. In actuality, how many of us deliberately consider this, and, of those who do, how many of us would even know how to begin to provide those basic needs for our children?

I believe we would live in a completely different kind of world if self-love and a strong dedication to altruism were in the forefront of our first two decades of life. I cannot speak for other cultures, but in America there is still very much a "Look out for #1" attitude. This is understandable, given the history of this country. A strong sense and historical influence of a "me-first" mentality is strongly embedded in the American declaration, "Independence for All." I think we have to take this at its literal meaning. This way of thinking has penetrated the way we raise our children, and every aspect of our daily lives. We value independence and selfhood far more than being there for others. We are less concerned about respect, love, and altruism and are choosing instead to put our energy and time into learning the skills or knowledge we need to get ahead of everyone else. In short, America is a caught up in the fast past race. For children with delays, this means that they are set behind already, and told to catch up as quickly as they can. This, of course, is sideways to the approaches I am asking you to begin working upon learning.

While we are raising perhaps the most productive, specialized, efficient human beings on the planet, our modernism has come at an extremely high cost. Our insatiable quest of the bigger, better, faster, stronger has taken precedence over that which makes us who we are—loving and caring people. Understanding and incorporating the social-emotional needs of every human being is at the core of The Social Diet. Our children's well-being should be guiding our child-rearing culture. It is the most important job of becoming a parent—to form a solid social/emotional foundation for our children.

How Can We Instill Love, Well-Being, And Altruism in Our Children?

The first needs are, of course, love and connection. All adults, all children, all beings need this, even those who are socially challenged. We may think that those with social cognitive challenges do not need others because they prefer to be on their own. They may think they like only being alone, but this isolation will cause them ill health.

How can we show love? First, it starts with the understanding of what each of us needs to thrive. Secondly, it requires us to understand that we are the role models for our children. We have to instill in our lives what we want to see in our children's lives. How can this be done? Below I describe some practical ways to model and instill love, well-being and kindness for our children. You can use the same techniques with yourself too. They work for anyone at any age at any time. The more time spent on this the better.

I start by using the above list of what every person needs at his/her core self and give some suggestions. – Remember for all of these needs all we have is our communication (verbal and non-verbal) to teach ourselves and our children our values and to show them that they are significant.

1. **We need to feel loved by others:** All children intrinsically know if they are loved. One important way to show love to our children is to make them feel like they truly matter and are important to us. We

can use our verbal language to show this by affirming your love several times a day, "I love you so much," "I am so happy you are in my life," "You make so happy," "You are so special to me" to name a few. Align your words with your non-verbal posturing and facial expressions. The more deliberate and sincere you are, the closer your child sense your sincerity and will want to be with you.

Do you need to use your words? Yes, and no. Sometimes saying nothing is even more powerful than using words. We all know this when we are in the arms of someone that we love and who loves us back. We want to show our kids that we love them through our body language and our non-verbal communication needs to align with our words. I also think we want to tell them this as well. I recognize that for some families this is easier than for others and can be influenced by peoples' culture and how they were raised as children. If telling your child that you love them does not come easily *that is okay*. Simply practice saying this every day, and it will be easier as time goes on. Say it with conviction in your heart and your child well feel the love.

I once read and article (and I can't recall which one unfortunately) but it described the way parents talk with their children. They reported that 85% of what parents say to their children is either what they need to do, or reprimanding them for what they are not doing. This leaves only 15% of our communication to express and share the positive things we see in our kids. Let's think about this. I often give my clients homework to do between our sessions. One of the first assignments is for them take simply take notice of what they are saying to their children and how they are saying it. I don't ask them to change anything, I just tell them to observe and become aware. (We can not change any behavior if we don't notice what we do first and understand why it might be important to change.) Inevitably they report back the same findings as the article states.

How many of us can thrive when we are constantly being told in an imperative command kind of way what to do or not do? Would we ourselves flourish under these conditions? No! None of us do well when we are getting mostly negative feedback throughout our day. Make a point to show your love and appreciation for your child every day, several times a day by telling them and showing them how important they are to you. I can guarantee that this will reinforce a close bond between the two of you. Any child will want to connect when they feel loved. Human nature is designed this way.

2. **We need to feel understood**. The strategies I suggest above can also apply much the same way here. It is important to use your words and your body language to express to your child that you hear them and understand them. We all need validation, especially our children so that they grow up thinking that they matter to you and others. We need to feel understood if we are to thrive in life. How many of us have experienced the frustration of not feeling understood? It can be exhausting not to mention humiliating. There will be so many innumerable times that you don't agree or like what your child is doing and/or saying. This is normal. Despite our instinct to again

jump in and tell them and show them that we disapprove, I invite you to take a different approach. Use empathy first.

If your child is showing signs of frustration, chances are he is not being heard or understood. You first job is to put yourself in your child's shoes and validate what they must be feeling by showing empathy. Use your words to reiterate what it is that you think is bothering them before you do or say anything else. For example, "I know you want to play with that toy and you don't like when I take it away." By saying this, you are validating their feelings or frustration of having to have their toy removed. Then come up with a solution that might work for both of you. For example, "I know you want to play with that toy and you don't like when I take it away. But you can play with it tonight again after dinner[8]."

3. **We need to feel accepted and that we belong**— All humans need to feel that we are wanted, accepted for who we are and the we all are a part of something that is bigger than ourselves. Each one of us has felt the bangs and pain of not being accepted at some or many instances throughout our lives. Feeling isolated and that we are different and therefore don't belong can and does have devastating consequences to our physical, social and emotional well-being. The science (and common sense) is there. Those who are shunned, made

1. [8] Then you need to take the toy away and bring it back after dinner as you had promised (unless your child is so misbehaved that he or she has lost this possibility.) You want your child to know that your word is your word and that you are consistently following through on what you say.

fun of, or simply do not fit into the mix, become our most vulnerable population. This is no little matter. In fact, it has so much significance in terms of how we see ourselves and how we show up for ourselves and others.

Make no mistake our children with ASD or related challenges are the most vulnerable. They have a severe risk of depression, anxiety and a plethora of other mental health conditions. This is also true for the typical population. Being and feeling isolated on top of not feeling accepted is at epidemic proportions. In some cases ignorance is bliss. But for the majority of our children, they want to feel accepted, they want to be included, they want to be liked. If they don't it's probably because they have not had enough positive experiences with others. I often see this. The child who is socially challenged makes attempt after attempt to try to fit in and make friends. Other children will always be able to pick up that our kids are different even if we can't see it. It is human nature to relinquish one's staying power if time and time again you are being rejected. I have seen mother's with heartache (myself included at one time) that their child is really trying to be social but others are not letting them inside their group. They need to know later in life that although they might be different they have just as many gifts and maybe more than others. Keep telling them how special they are, how much they are loved and then create environments and experiences with people that support this. Yes, this is work and it takes deliberate action on your part. But again, this is a core need that must be provided for your child to thrive. This is why the previous chapter of building friendship and community is so important in your life and your children's lives. We need to give our children the love and knowledge that they do belong just the way they are.

4. We need to feel safe. When it comes to our safety we are referring to safety both in the realms of the physical and emotional. You need to show both at the same time. Sometimes we might forget that our children when they are young are very fragile emotionally. They learn from a very early age whom they can trust and who they can't. The more secure they feel emotionally, the better our kids do. Emotions are a tricky business and not at all straight forward for any young child or for any individual if they have not had healthy role models to take after. Their behavior is often a direct product of what they have been exposed to in their environment. Are they feeling physically and emotionally safe when they are with you? How can you tell?

All children will give you the feedback you are seeking. If you know what to look for (how your child acts and expresses him/herself when they are feeling secure as opposed to how they are behaving when they are feeling vulnerable.) The clues lie in our children's behavior. What they say or do, or don't say or don't do is directly impacted by the kinds of environments they live in. Often your children might act out because they are not feeling safe.

Please understand that your child is acting out for a reason. Behaviors do not happen in a vacuum. I can guarantee that when our children act out it is because their needs are not being met. Besides needing the basics of food, shelter, water, the reason for most tantrums is because we, the adult, have not figured out the missing piece. All six human needs I am presenting have got to be addressed. You want to ask yourself, "Am I providing the six essential needs for my child? Go down the list and see what might be missing from his/her Social Diet.

The key for our children to feel emotionally and physically safe is for us, the adults in their lives to demonstrate regulation in yourself. We have already mentioned earlier that if you are in a reactive state, mostly likely your child will match your state. The same is true if you exude a sense of calm and peace. Once again it is our choice of how we use our verbal and non-verbal language. You know the expression, "Monkey see, monkey do!"

Our environments also refer to one's physical (outside) environment (where you are such as at school, at home, on the playground,) and the internal or emotional environments of which reside with the people (and context) your children are with.

5. **We need to feel certainty and…**

6. **We need to feel uncertainty**—To some degree this human need is related to feeling safe and secure like the one above, but they are different. Despite our need for novelty (discussed below) on some level human beings have to have a sense of control in their lives. We do need to have certain aspects of our daily lives to be stable or we can become emotionally dysregulated or unstable.

Some uncertainty or novelty is necessary- While what I said is true, we want to be careful not to give our kids too much certainty all day long every day. I have seen parents (and other professionals) want to cater to our children's desire to keep things the same way and will do so in the vein of keeping their child feeling okay and for their child to know what is expected and what to expect. Keeping things the same day after day leads to fewer behavioral outbursts. Like we discussed earlier, our children who tend to be more dysregulated than most, prefer predictable habits and situations.

The caveat here as was stated earlier in the book, is that if we keep everything the same our kids will not have the experiences they need to be okay when things do not turn out the way that they expect. I will give you and example of a client I had. He was about nine years old. His parents thought they were helping him by keeping his schedule the same everyday. He woke up at 7:00am, got dressed and either played a bit or got ready for school. Breakfast was at 7:30am. Then either the bus came for school or he knew on the weekends that he could watch TV. His entire day was scheduled as close as possible to be the same everyday. One night when I was there, Charley rushed into the kitchen and stared at the clock. It was 4:54pm. He knew it was dinner time at precisely 5:00pm. Not one minute before and not one minute after. When I asked his parents about this, they confirmed that Charley likes his dinner at 5:00 each night and has made it known that if he doesn't get his dinner then, there will be trouble (a major meltdown.) Obviously, his parents wanted to avoid this at all costs so they catered to their son's needs time and time again.

If we really think about this, we can see that this might not be serving Charley in the long run. How many of us have control over anything and everything that happens in our lives? I don't know anyone who does and I would bet that neither do you. Again, I have mentioned this throughout the book, we need to consider what our child will need when they are an adult. We have to prepare them for that even when they are only two, three, and four years old. While some degree of certainty is warranted, do not keep your child's schedules, routines and experiences the same. You want to mix things up, change the way you do things, where you go, how you play a game together. The more opportunities our children have to understand that flexibility (change) is a normal part of life, the better off our adult children will learn how to deal with the uncertainty of real life. I am not suggesting that you create chaos for your kids. They do need a certain amount of stability but enough instability to be able to cope with other people's and other environmental factors that are out of our control. This leads us to our next human need.

It's true. Life would be rather boring and we would remain stagnant if we didn't experience some degree of newness. I think a lot of us realize that people are supposed to be perpetually growing and learning and experiencing new things. Again, human nature is designed this way. We really do have richer lives when we immerse ourselves in learning about new things and new people. We don't live in a vacuum, nor should we. The same is true for our children.

They may act like they want things to remain the same as in the above example with Charley, but I can predict that either they will become bored or become stifled or both. Again, you as the parent will want to go out of your way to add newness and new experiences in your child's life. The degree to which they rebel is indicative of just how stuck they have become. This again is why The Social Diet is easier to practice the younger your child is. If you have a teenager already with whom you never really introduced new situations and problems that needed solutions, my advice to you is to start with small tolerable changes. This simply could mean taking one different street from the one you normally take. Of it could mean introducing one more food a week that your child isn't familiar with. Again, we don't want to make colossal changes all at once. We want to gradually introduce novelty in little doses. This will require you the parent to be strong and not to give in. You want to give your child the opportunity to realize that even though something was not done the way he wanted, he survived in the end. Nothing terrible happened. He might (re)act like something terrible is happening, but unless his physical well being is compromised, be persistent and know that he or she will survive. In fact the more opportunity to practice living in uncertainty, they better they will be equipped as adults to deal with whatever life throws their way. Most of us have heard the phrase, "Life is what happens between the plans." Wouldn't you rather expose your child to novel situations when he or she is young rather than to wait until they are adults and have not had the support when they were younger to have the flexibility of thinking and acting they now need. Think about how important a gift you can give your child that things might not stay the same, but that is okay because you are there to show them how to cope with this and move on to a healthier and more realistic lifestyle.

Reflection and Questions:

• Spend a few days observing your verbal and non-verbal communication. How much of that time are you reinforcing how wonderful your child is, and how much you love him/her and how much you appreciate them being in your life? Below write down your thoughts and what you are noticing about your own behavior and that of your child.

• In a week's time try to deliberately practice the strategies above. What differences have you noticed in yourself and your child?

• Do the same exercise after 3 more weeks, (so a month from the time you first noticed the kind of feedback you give your child). What are you noticing now? Write down what you have been experiencing.

• Just for fun try showing up by using different types of emotions when you are with your child. For example, approach your child with a calming gentle warm tone. Then use a reactive voice and strong body language of disapproval. On another occasion show up laughing, and show up crying. What do you notice? What do you notice about your child's behavior based on your own? Write down your thoughts.

• Think back to a time in your childhood where you felt disconnected or isolated from others. How did it feel? What did you do or not do because of this? Were any opportunities lost?

• Now think of the same thing but this time think about a time in your adulthood when you felt like you didn't fit in and were not accepted by others. What was the specific situation?

• What were the circumstances?

• What were the direct outcomes for feeling this way?

• What could you or others have done to make you feel accepted and included?

Are you providing the same opportunities for your child? How do you make your child feel accepted? Are you doing it enough? Please explain and give details.

List 10 things in your life that are predictable:

1.

2.

3.

4.

5.

6.

7.

8.

9.

10.

List 10 things in your life that are unpredictable:

1.

2.

3.

4.

5.

6.

7.

8.

9.

10.

• In what kinds of ways does your need for certainty play a role in your life and life style? What are the benefits you get from things you can rely on? Can you give some examples?

• In what kinds of ways does *un*certainty play a role in your life and lifestyle? What are the specific and general benefits you might experience from being someone that embraces newness or uncertainty?

• In what ways could creating uncertainty for your child be beneficial in general terms and in specific terms?

• What things might you try to insert in your child's life to enrich it with new experiences?

List up to 10 things you would like your child to be more flexible with.

1.

2.

3.

4.

5.

6.

7.

8.

9.

10.

• Finally, what would your life, your child's life and the life of your family look like if you were able to teach him/her how to cope with uncertainty?

• How would your lives be different?

• How would the quality of life change for all of you?

• Please explain and give details.

Next Steps: How to Incorporate The Social Diet® into Your Everyday Life?

Having Knowledge is Not Enough. Using The ADCAR Model

Now that you have read all about The Social Diet and its essential ingredients, what is next? The knowledge you gained is not enough. It is only the first step.

For real and sustainable change to happen (meaning factors influencing success)- in this case raising well-balanced, socially connected and, caring kids, 5 things need to be in place. They are:

1. **Awareness** of the need to change
2. **Desire** to support and participate in the change
3. **Knowledge** of how to change
4. **Ability** to implement required skills and behaviors
5. **Reinforcement** to sustain the changes

I take this directly from the ADKAR[9] model. ADCAR uses the above five elements as building blocks for change to happen. It is wonderful that you have taken the time to read The Social Diet. But you must not stop there. If you want you and your family to make sustainable changes, all five of the ADKAR elements must be used

---

[9] Jeffery M. Hiatt, ADKAR: A MODEL FOR CHANGE IN BUSINESS, GOVERNMENT AND OUR COMMUNITY. How to Implement Successful Change in Our Personal Lives and Professional Careers. Prosci Learning Center Publications, Loveland, Colorado. 2006.

and incorporated to be successful with The Social Diet long term. The above 5 elements are straight forward. I hope I have given ample examples of why you need to be more aware of your own behavior first. You must then have a desire to want to change and be given the appropriate knowledge to know how to implement the changes. Next this requires that you receive the required skills that give you the ability to implement the new behaviors. Lastly, is the reinforcement stage. You need to practice The Social Diet on a daily basis. The more you practice, the better off you and your child will be.

• CHAPTER 6 •

Conclusion

Parenting Onward With The Social Diet

Parenting is the most difficult job in the world, even with the best and "easiest" kids. To me, shaping another human life is more important, and more honorable, than any other kind of work on this planet. As my mother used to say, "Anything worthwhile is not easy." Most of us have to work at parenting, day in and day out. While there might be amazing peaks, there are definitely valleys, too. I don't know any parent who hasn't said to him or herself, "*Why exactly* did I want kids?" For those who are raising special need children it is even tougher and sometimes downright unbearable to learn how to parent these unique individuals. The amount of time, effort, energy, responsibility and love it takes to parent a special needs kid is endless. But…so is our ability to love, and learn and grow in our parenting techniques in order to help our child learn this new, foreign language of our culture and society.

While the demands of our current culture, "Do more, assimilate more, faster, better," prevails, we literally are being pushed to our limits of energy and patience, and then pushed onward some more. In the business world, we are asked to perform at an unprecedented speed, often without awareness of how all of this is affecting our personal well-being, our relationships, and our home life. Some of you may be thinking, “What home life? I don’t *have* a home life.” How many times do you ask people how they are doing, and their response is “Busy. Too busy.” I call this the “Too busy” generation.

The “Too busy” generation spans across all ages, and doesn’t discriminate by race, gender, income level, or status. We are all victims of it. We all experience it everyday, every week, and every year. The frightening part is that I don’t see this trend ending, not soon or ever. In fact, I see symptoms getting worse.

It’s easy to be too busy to have time for what the research has proven, time and time again—that relationships and community are the key to living a more fulfilling and happy life. We persist in being Too Busy-- too busy to be available for our most important asset we will ever have in life, our children. But, what is more important than our children? We may say the answer is nothing, but, we as a culture are showing by our actions that this is not the case. On average, we are spending less and less time with our kids and more time at our jobs.

The foundation of The Social Diet is that parents and caregivers need to become more deliberate, more thoughtful, more aware about how they live their lives in a balanced and healthy way while fostering a home environment that is loving, caring, mentally healthy, and where there is time to be together to create and experience life together as a team. Nothing, let me repeat, *nothing* can take the place of this kind of family life. Not the best gadget, or best device, or any entertainment known to man. The foundation to human health is a healthy home life where all members of the family feel loved, understood, protected, safe, heard, accepted and significant. This is hard to accomplish given how most of us live our lives.

What would it need to take for you to be able to provide this kind of environment for yourself and others?

This may be an uncomfortable question, but that doesn't mean we should avoid it. Quite the contrary. Remember, if you are bold enough to take this question on, you must recall the mindsets in chapter 4. What is your mindset regarding making changes to your life and/or your family's lives? I urge you to do whatever it takes to make sure that there is more than *financial* stability in your home. Despite the American dream, which we still seem to want, money does not make a life. Connections and communications with people do.

Before I end, I would like to share another letter from my son that was written four years after the letter you read in Chapter one. You see, my family and I continue to work on The Social Diet every day. It never stops just like parenting never stops. It is never easy just like parenting is never easy. It's not supposed to be. Guiding a well fed life of balance, love and connection takes time, even years. But what else are we parents here for, if not for our children? I have created The Social Diet to be an integral part of us and how we choose to parent. In essence The Social Diet is a lifestyle choice that brings to our attention to and teaches us what our most important beliefs and values are and how we can live a life that supports and sustains this way of living- a connected healthy lifestyle where we take care of ourselves and each other. Wouldn't we want to choose this and be able to model it and pass it down for our children, and our children's children? In the end it is our human birthright to choose how we want to live and choose with whom we live it.

Over time, The Social Diet will become a habit, where you don't have to think about what to do or how to do it. It will begin to seem so natural that you will feel the true gifts and joys of social-oriented parenting. You will feel proud that you have taken the time to set your own priorities, and those of your family. You will be proud that you have built a life that feeds and nourishes all of you in a healthy and balanced way. You will feel confident that you have given your children more than enough experiences to create the solid emotional foundation which they can build upon. You will feel peace in knowing that you taught them how to create and nurture relationships, which have taught them how to feel connected, seek out others and have empathy towards other people.

Yes, all the hard work does pay off, if you have a determined and empowered mindset. If you are persistent, you will be just fine…and even thrive!

I'm closing with the second letter which Ylann has written to me, this time for Mother's Day in May 2018. I could not fathom a letter like this 15 years ago. All of us could live with a steady diet of this kind of love from our children, especially those who have a great deal of difficulty expressing themselves. I share this with you not to brag about how great my son is (which he is), but to show you that living The Social Diet lifestyle is possible. The rewards are endless.

My hope for your family is immense, and I hope you can feel it, too. May each passing day bring you closer together. May each of you live a life which is balanced. May each of you live a life that matters and brings love, joy and peace to ourselves and to all those we have touched, and whom have touched us, along this magnificent journey of life.

Mother's Day Card

(5/12/18)

Dear Mom,

Thank you so much for everything, it means a lot. Everyone in the family loves and respects you, especially me even though sometimes I don't show it. Embrace what you love the most; me and Yael. Feel the sensations that make us one. Break the objects that seize us apart. I love you so much and it is an honor, an honor to have you as my Mom. No matter what anyone says, you are the go to enterprise of my life. I have faith that you will become successful and I know you will always find a way to enlighten and empower people around you. You are special and I always want you to remember me, even when you die. I will always remember you. I love you, Mom.

Sincerely, Ylann Goresko

#Be the one.

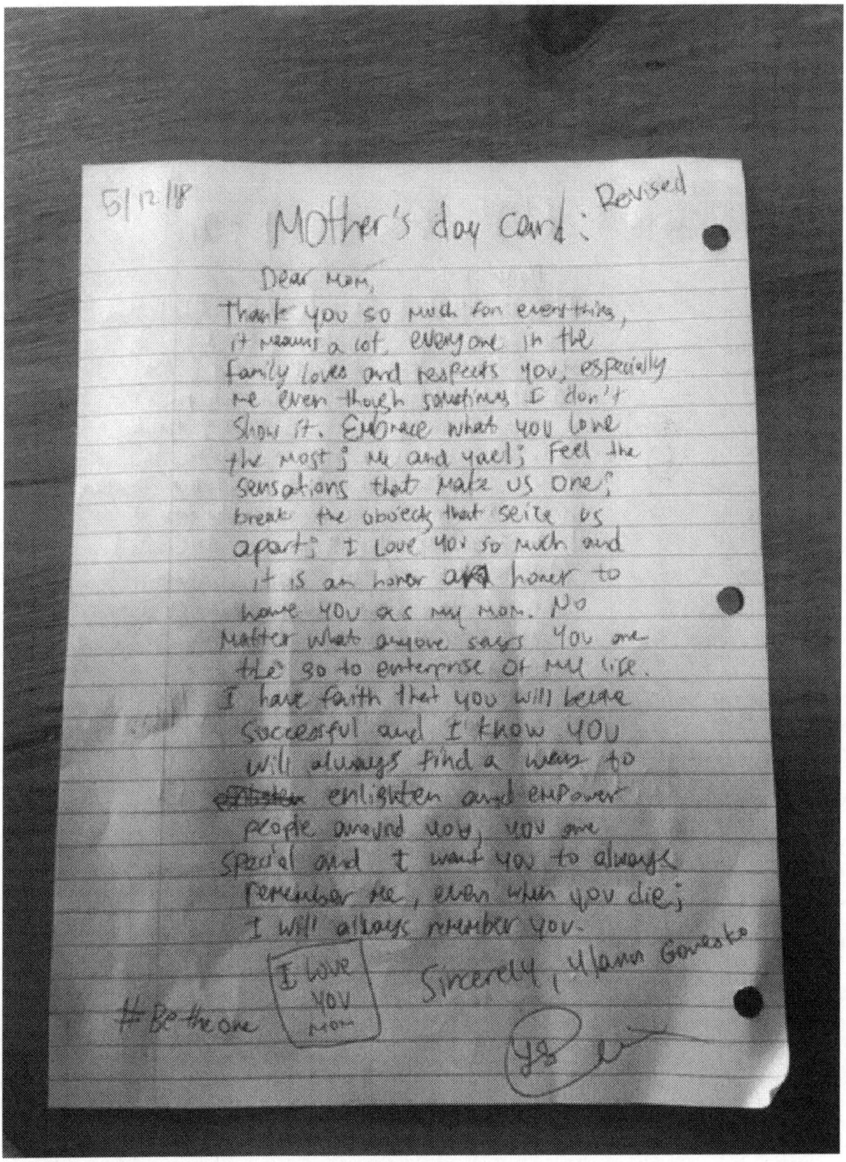

5/12/18

Mother's day card: Revised

Dear Mom,

Thank you so much for everything, it means a lot, everyone in the family loves and respects you, especially me even though sometimes I don't show it. Embrace what you love the most; me and yael; Feel the sensations that make us one; break the obstacles that seize us apart; I love you so much and it is an honor and honer to have you as my mom. No matter what anyone says you are the go to enterprise of my life. I have faith that you will become successful and I know you will always find a way to enlighten and empower people around you, you are special and I want you to always remember me, even when you die; I will always member you.

Sincerely, Ilana Goresko

I love you Mom

#Be the one

It is my sincere dream that *The Social Diet*→ will bring forth a revolutionary way/path to raise socially-connected, balanced, and caring kids in the generations to come. I want the lives of all our children to be joyful and meaningful in a way that feeds their souls.

• CHAPTER 7 •

Frequently Asked Questions about The Social Diet

Does The Social Diet Work?

As I stated in the beginning of this book, I cannot predict what will work for you and your child. I can tell you however that without a steady social diet, your child will never reach his social potential. I have found, however, great success for my own family and those of my clients. As your only expense to learn these steps has been that of purchasing this book, I encourage you to put the simple techniques into practice in your home. It will only work, if you do.

How Often Should I Practice The Social Diet?

As with any new habit you are trying to adopt, I suggest starting out slowly, but steadily. At first you just want to get your feet wet. Once you feel comfortable with the beginning steps, you will want to do more. You want to set yourself up for success, so choose an amount of time that is both possible to initiate and sustain. I recommend you only do 10 minutes per day for five days during your first two weeks.

On week three, build up to 20 minutes a day for five days. About week six, go for 30 minutes per day for five days. Once you feel comfortable with that, build up to an hour or more per day, five times a week. You are building your muscles here. Once this style of communication becomes part of your routine, you will be doing it without even realizing it.

What if we miss a day or two or even a week?

Don't worry about it! In life, things get in the way and we can't always get to everything we need to do. Just don't give up. Pick it back up in a day or two. Just know that results do vary. Each family is different, and their practice in learning new communication styles will be different as well. However, the more committed you are, the faster and better results you will have.

Can any child make progress when on The Social Diet?

Yes. Both neurotypical and non-neurotypical children can benefit greatly from it. Even if your child is considered to be "low-functioning," you and your child will make gains from The Social Diet. Every child, including those on the spectrum, is capable of developing deeper connections with others. I've seen some families with low-functioning children improve more in the social arena than some of their "higher-functioning" counterparts. While you cannot predict how far your child will go with The Social Diet, if you do not embed the social piece into your children's daily lives, they have little chance of ever being proficient at social communication. The more your child understands and participates in the social world, and the more you are a part of making this happen, the further your child will progress.

What about if my child is non-verbal? Can The Social Diet still work for us?

Yes, most definitely! In fact, I have found that spoken language can actually hinder social connections. We've discussed how only 15 percent of communication is verbal. The other 85 percent is non-verbal (body language, facial expressions, tone of voice, physical environment, context), and your child likely reads your non-verbal communication better than you realize. What this means is that even not-NT children who are strong verbally are lacking the other 85 percent of communication. Without a foundation in non-verbal behavior, a child will not be able to partake in the natural flow of back and forth communication. So, teaching non-verbal communication is where I put a lot of emphasis. I teach parents how to communicate with their children *without* using words. Words can act as a crutch. When we take the words away, it forces the child to have to pick up important contextual information that they will need to figure out if they are ever going to be an appropriate social partner. So, although it might seem counterintuitive, those children who are non-verbal may make more initial progress with The Social Diet than their verbal counterparts.

Do both parents need to participate?

No, they don't. However, I believe your child will benefit more if both parents participate in The Social Diet. Remember, The Social Diet requires that you change the way you behave and communicate with your child. It is best if both parents learn to do that in a similar fashion so that your styles match one another. There is more opportunity for consistency this way. Also, if you both do it your child gets more exposure and practice doing the diet. It would be ideal if both parents, child care workers, grandparents, and any other adult who spends time with your child learns how to do The Social Diet.

Many of us, however, do not have that kind of family support and cooperation. Often it is only one parent, or a single parent, who is available to put the commitment and time into learning how to do The Social Diet. Rest assured that you and your child will still benefit. It is much better to be doing The Social Diet some of the time, than none of the time. So, even if your child can only learn from one person, this still can make a significant difference.

Is The Social Diet Solely a Home-Based Approach?

Definitely not! Practicing The Social Diet at home is easier because you don't have the constraints of a classroom, but ideally The Social Diet can be taught in *any* setting. With the proper mindset and support, I think anyone can provide a more socially-based learning environment, including schools.

Is The Social Diet just for kids with Autism Spectrum Disorder?

No, it isn't. I think of The Social Diet when I think of autism because my personal experience and clientele tend to be someplace on the spectrum, but most everyone in this population struggles with social relationships in one way or another. There are, however, a number of other populations, with or without diagnosis, which need help navigating and participating in the social world. I use The Social Diet with my NT daughter, and with any child in general. By practicing The Social Diet, our neurotypical children can learn why we adults think and act like we do. It gives them a better understanding of empathy, perspective taking, and collaboration.

Appendix

The Role of Parents: Where to Begin? What to do?

Before getting a diagnosis:

Scenario 1

You have a gut feeling that something may be wrong or different about your child.

What should you do?

> **Answer**: Trust your instincts. If you think there is something not quite right, do something about it--even if your partner, family, teachers, doctors, or professionals tell you otherwise. They don't know your child like you do. While their opinions matter, they can be wrong.

Scenario 2

You, your partner or other professionals are indicating, "Yes, your child is a little behind or different but let's wait and see what happens…"

> **Answer**: Do not wait. Some things do not matter if you play the "wait and see" game. However,

for a possible developmental delay, the sooner you find out, the better.

Scenario 3

You are told that your child does have a developmental delay. Now what?

Answer: If you do get some difficult news, *don't bury your head in the sand.* As much as you may wish and hope that circumstances were different, you don't want to waste any time. If you need to get a second opinion, do so. However, the faster you act, and the earlier you start to receive services and get the support you need, the better off your child will be in their progress towards adulthood. It is far better to err on the side of needing help, than pretending nothing is wrong. I recognize receiving a diagnosis is an enormous blow to you and your family. You've read what my experience with the grief cycle was like, and how hard it was for our family to progress through it. If you are having difficulties managing this news, please seek out professional help to support you. The healthier you are, the more available you will be for your child. There is no shame in asking for help, and no sorrow in recognizing that you still need to learn and grow as a parent, and as a human. We all do.

After Getting a Diagnosis: Now what?

Understand that you need to be at the helm of your child's life, both at home and at school. It's difficult to learn to advocate for both yourself and for your child. We live in a society where we are told to sit back and not worry, because the professionals are in charge. Others can support you and should, but ultimately you (and your partner) have the ultimate responsibility for your child when it comes to choosing services. You have to educate yourself and your support people, so you can make powerful and informed decisions. Talk to as many people as you can, read as much as you can and become a discerning and discriminatory consumer.

Invest in yourself. Doctors, therapists, teachers, and professionals will come and go in your child's life, but you are there for the long term. Do not rely on others to save you, or replace you. Spend your time, energy, and resources on getting educated so that you can come become the expert on what your child needs. Talk to as many parents, professionals, and doctors as you can, but in the end, do what makes the most sense for you and your family.

Remember, your child is not his or her label.

We never let Ylann's autism define who he is, nor who I am. I think the best advice I ever received, at the start of our autism journey, came from a mother who had a teenager with autism. She said to me, "Looking back, I wish I had remembered that he was just a little boy. I spent so much of my time driving from one therapy appointment to the next, that I didn't get a chance to just enjoy him." I appreciated her telling me this and it made me put things into perspective. Yes, Ylann had autism, but he was still my precious Ylann, and I wanted to devote as much time as I possibly could with him.

1. Make the relationship which you build with your child your top priority (after any medical issues, of course). Put your time into establishing a close, intimate, loving, and caring relationship with your child.

2. Understand the legal rights of your special-needs child. The law is often on your side. Talk to other parents, and find out what services they have been eligible for. Sometimes government agencies will cover various fees, but if you don't ask them directly what kind of funding is available, they might not disclose important services that your child may be entitled to.

3. Set the highest expectations, and never think that your child can't do or learn something.

4. Trust your instincts. If you think there is something not quite right, do something about it even if the doctors or professionals tell you otherwise. They don't know your child like you do. While their opinions matter, they can be wrong. Don't play the "Let's wait and see what happens game." Seek out others' opinions.

5. Surround yourself with family and friends. You cannot manage this yourself—none of us can! Asking for help is not a sign of weakness; it actually shows great courage. People want to help, but you do need to ask. For some people, and in some cultures, asking for help is extremely difficult or not easily accepted. While I respect that, it really does take a community to embrace and support you as a special-needs family. You are just at beginning this journey, and you will need the support of others.

6. It is your job, and no one else's, to teach your child how to behave in social situations and in community relationships. Do not look solely to the schools to do this job. They are there to teach your child to do other things. There is no getting around this. Do the behavioral

groundwork before your child develops poor habits that will become harder and harder to extinguish later.

7.Learn and teach what your goals, values, and desires are for your child, and make those your priorities. Spend your time on the important parts (relationship building) and don't waste your energy on things that don't matter as much in the short term.

8. Create your own definition of success: What does a successful life look like and feel like to you? What does that look like for your child?

9. Create a life of balance.

10. Laugh a lot, love a lot and have fun experiences together!

Acknowledgments

It truly does take a village. I could not have written this book without the love and support of my family, friends and community. There are so many of you who have cheered me on throughout this project, and I am forever grateful. Thank you to my editors, Amy Collette, Heather Harris-Bergevin and Carol Stein, my readers Barbara Hess, Camille Kolu and Murrie Gayman, and everyone else who offered suggestions. I want to thank my intern, Allie Datz. In addition, I want to thank all of my beloved neighbors who stepped in at all times of day to lend me a shoulder or a hand. I want to thank my entire family (Lou, Moo, and Drue)--I did it! Thanks to the heartfelt love and support I was able to accomplish my dream.

Aunt Carol, this is for you.

Mom, our daily morning pep talks will forever be imprinted in my heart. Thanks for being such a great role model for me. I am the kind of mother I am because of you.

Dad, I get my creative visionary side from you. You have always taught me to find my passion and believe in myself.

Gaye, you have been with me since the day we met and still are. You were my earthly angel for too brief a time. I know you are proud of me and smiling down on me.

I want to especially thank you, Glen. You have believed in me from day one even when I doubted myself. You have been the wind beneath my wings. Your unconditional love is a true gift to me. Thank you.

About the Author

Stacy Goresko, Ph.D., is an accomplished Author, Speaker, Trainer, Certified Autism Consultant and Inspirational Life Coach. Most importantly, she is a mother of two, one of whom is on the Autism Spectrum. Born and raised in Philadelphia, Stacy now resides with her two children in Boulder, Colorado. She has made it her mission in life to bring people together and create meaningful relationships and community. When you don't see her being Mom or helping others, you will find her hiking in the Rockies, riding her horse or simply enjoying the wonders of nature.

If you would like to learn more about Dr. Goresko and The Social Diet, please visit www.TheSocialDiet.com.

If you would like to hire Dr. Goresko for speaking, training, consulting, or to learn how to become a Social Diet Practitioner, she can be reached at Stacy@TheSocialDiet.com.

Notes:

32658101R00126

Made in the USA
Columbia, SC
06 November 2018